113–114

Editorial:
Automatic affective processing

Jan De Houwer

University of Southampton, UK

Dirk Hermans

University of Leuven, Belgium

The concepts "affect", "valence", and "attitude" are all fundamentally linked to the basic psychological dimension of good vs. bad, positive vs. negative, approach vs. avoid. With "affective processing" we mean the processing of stimulus valence, that is, the act of determining the location of a stimulus on the affective dimension. Over the past few decades, scholars of emotion theory (e.g., Sherer, 1993), social psychology (e.g., Zajonc, 1980, 1984), and learning psychology (e.g., Martin & Levey, 1978) have put forward the hypothesis that affective processing does not depend on controlled cognitive processing. That is, they proposed that organisms are able to determine whether a stimulus is good or bad without engaging in intentional, goal-directed, conscious, or capacity-demanding processing of the (evaluative attributes of the) stimulus. Rather, affective processing could occur automatically. Such automatic affective processing was believed to have an important impact on subsequent cognitive processing and behaviour (e.g., Zajonc, 1980, 1984).

These proposals led to a multitude of research. New paradigms were developed that allow one to study the conditions under which stimulus valence can be processed and efforts were directed at understanding how such affective processing influences subsequent cognitive processing and behaviour. The aim of this Special Issue is to provide an overview of some of: (a) the paradigms that are available to study automatic affective processing, (b) the knowledge about affective processing that has been gained over the last several years, and (c) the issues and questions that are currently being addressed and that will most likely dominate the research in the years to come. Of course, not all aspects of recent research on automatic affective processing can be addressed in this Issue.

Correspondence should be addressed to Dr Jan De Houwer, Department of Psychology, University of Southampton, Highfield, Southampton. SO17 1BJ, UK; e-mail: JanDH@soton.ac.uk.

© 2001 Psychology Press Ltd

http://www.tandf.co.uk/journals/pp/02699931.html   DOI:10.1080/0269993004200015

Nevertheless, we hope that it provides a useful introduction to this fascinating research area.

This Special Issue grew out of a workshop that took place 16 December 1998 at the University of Leuven, Belgium. The workshop was made possible by the financial support of the Fund for Scientific Research (Flanders, Belgium) as part of the Scientific Research Network "Acquisition and Representation of Evaluative Judgements and Emotions". Neither the workshop, nor the Special Issue could have been realised without the constant help and inspiration provided by Paul Eelen.

Manuscript received 22 February 2000

REFERENCES

Martin, I., & Levey, A.B. (1978). Evaluative conditioning. *Advances in Behaviour Research and Therapy*, *1*, 57–102.

Sherer, K.R. (1993). Neuroscience projections to current debates in emotion psychology. *Cognition and Emotion*, *7*, 1–42.

Zajonc, R.B. (1980). Feeling and thinking. Preferences need no inferences. *American Psychologist*, *35*, 151–175.

Zajonc, R.B. (1984). On the primacy of affect. *American Psychologist*, *39*, 117–123.

COGNITION AND EMOTION, 2001, *15* (2), 115–141

On the automatic activation of associated evaluations: An overview

Russell H. Fazio

Indiana University, Bloomington, USA

A review of the literature concerning the phenomenon known as automatic attitude activation is presented. The robustness of the affective priming effect across many different procedural variations, the mediating mechanisms thought to underlie the effect, and the moderating role of associative strength are discussed. The relevance and importance of automatic attitude activation to many fundamental cognitive and social processes also is highlighted. Finally, an overview of the articles included in this Special Issue of *Cognition and Emotion*, their essential contributions, and their relation to the earlier literature is presented.

This Special Issue is devoted to furthering our understanding of a phenomenon known as automatic attitude activation. Essentially, presentation of an attitude object has been shown to automatically activate from memory the evaluation that an individual associates with the object. The editors Jan De Houwer and Dirk Hermans have compiled a collection of interesting articles in which the various contributing authors report investigations relevant to this phenomenon. In this introductory article, I will provide a brief overview of the articles in the special issue, as well as the literature on automatic attitude activation. In so doing, I hope to provide a context for the Special Issue and, even more importantly, an appreciation for the significance of the phenomenon.

The affective priming effect

Much of the research on attitude activation has employed a priming paradigm that is itself a variant of classic priming research concerned with spreading activation processes. This classic work focused on lexical decisions, or more

Correspondence should be addressed to Russell H. Fazio, Department of Psychology, Indiana University, Bloomington, IN 47405; e-mail: Fazio@indiana.edu.

Preparation of this article was supported by Senior Scientist Award MH01646 and Grant MH38832 from the National Institute of Mental Health. The author thanks Jan De Houwer, Michael Olson, and Tamara Towles-Schwen for their helpful comments on an earlier version of the manuscript.

http://www.tandf.co.uk/journals/pp/02699931.html   DOI:10.1080/0269993004200024

specifically, on the latency with which such word/nonword judgements were made and the extent to which they were facilitated by the prior presentation of a prime. The findings of numerous experiments indicated that lexical decisions for concepts associated with the prime were facilitated by exposure to the prime (e.g., Meyer & Schvaneveldt, 1971; Neely, 1976, 1977). Thus, presentation of "doctor" as a prime facilitated identification of "nurse" as a word. The findings suggested that concepts associated with the prime are automatically activated from memory on its presentation (Schneider & Shiffrin, 1977; Shiffrin & Schneider, 1977) and, hence, facilitate responding to semantically related target words.

Motivated by their model of attitudes as object-evaluation associations in memory, Fazio, Sanbonmatsu, Powell, and Kardes (1986) reasoned that a similar priming effect should be apparent for attitudes. Presentation of the attitude object as a prime should activate any associated evaluations and, hence, facilitate a related judgement. The paradigm that Fazio et al. (1986) developed, and that has been employed in much of the subsequent research, involved the participants' performance on an adjective connotation task. The target word presented on each trial was an evaluative adjective and the participants were instructed to indicate whether the word meant "good" or "bad" as quickly as possible. The focus was on the latency with which this judgement was made and, in particular, the extent to which it was facilitated by the presentation of an attitude object as a prime.

In three experiments, Fazio et al. (1986) found evidence of automatic attitude activation. Under certain conditions, responding was faster on trials for which the participants' evaluations of the primed attitude objects were congruent with the connotation of the targets than on trials for which they were incongruent. To provide an example, assume that the attitude object "cockroach" is evaluated negatively by an individual. Presentation of "cockroach" as the prime appears to automatically activate the negative evaluation. If the target adjective that is subsequently presented is also negative (e.g., "disgusting"), then the individual is able to indicate the connotation of the target adjective relatively quickly, more so than if a positive adjective (e.g., "appealing") serves as the target word. A reverse pattern of facilitation is observed for primed objects that are associated with a positive evaluation. Thus, a significant interaction between the valence of the prime and the valence of the target is the hallmark of the automatic activation effect.

It is important to keep in mind that the priming procedure employed by Fazio et al. (1986) did not require participants to consciously evaluate the primes. From the perspective of the participants, the primes were being presented as "memory words" for the purpose of increasing the complexity of the adjective connotation task. Participants were instructed to remember and recite the memory word aloud at the end of the trial, after having pressed the "good" or "bad" key to indicate the connotation of the target adjective. Thus, participants were not asked to consider their attitudes toward the primes during the priming task. Nor was it to the participants' advantage to do so, for their major task assignment was to respond to the target adjective. Moreover, positively valued and negatively valued primes were equally likely to be followed by the presentation of a positive or a negative target. Thus, any attempts to predict the valence of the upcoming target on the basis of the prime would be futile.[1] Despite the irrelevance of the prime to the immediate task concerns, the prime influenced the ease with which participants could indicate the connotation of the target adjectives. Thus, the key nature of the task suggests that primes exerted their influence through an automatic process.

More importantly, the experiments revealed the automatic activation of attitudes only when the time interval between presentation of the prime and target was relatively brief—a stimulus onset asynchrony (SOA) of 300 ms. No such effect was apparent at an SOA of 1000 ms. Yet, if the results had been due to a more strategic, controlled, and effortful process, one would have expected that allotting the participants more time to actively retrieve their attitudes toward the primes would have, if anything, enhanced the facilitation effect. Instead, the findings imply that the evaluation associated with the prime received some activation automatically as a result of the prime's presentation, which facilitated responding to evaluatively congruent targets that were presented very soon thereafter. However, the level of activation must have either dissipated quickly, or been actively suppressed due to its presumed irrelevance to the primary task of judging the target adjective. Similar effects of setting the SOA at 300 versus 1000 ms have been observed in subsequent research (e.g., De Houwer, Hermans, & Eelen, 1998; Hermans, De Houwer, & Eelen, 1994). That is, the evaluative congruency of the prime and target mattered only at the shorter SOA.

The affective priming effect has been observed in numerous subsequent experiments. It has proven to be a robust and replicable phenomenon apparent in experiments using a variety of priming stimuli, target stimuli, and specific task requirements. The effect has been found when the words serving as primes are presented subliminally (e.g., Greenwald, Draine, & Abrams, 1996; Greenwald, Klinger, & Liu, 1989; Wittenbrink, Judd, & Park, 1997), further attesting to its characterisation as an automatic process. Moreover, evidence of automatic attitude activation has been demonstrated in later experiments, not only with the names of familiar attitude objects serving as primes (e.g., Bargh, Chaiken, Govender, & Pratto, 1992), but also with so-called "Turkish words" whose translation had been learned in an earlier phase of the experiment (De Houwer et

---

[1] See Klauer, Roßnagel, and Musch (1997) for research concerning the effects of varying the proportion of evaluatively congruent primes and targets.

al., 1998), with black-and-white line drawings of objects (Giner-Sorolla, Garcia, & Bargh, 1999), and with high-resolution colour images of the objects (e.g., Fazio, 1993; Fazio, Jackson, Dunton, & Williams, 1995; Hermans et al., 1994). The effect even has been observed across stimulus modalities. In an intriguing experiment conducted by Hermans, Baeyens, and Eelen (1998), positive or negative odours that had been idiosyncratically selected for each participant served as primes. The odours facilitated responses to visually presented target words that were affectively congruent.

The affective priming effect also has been observed in experiments using a variety of target stimuli. Much of the research has employed evaluative adjectives as targets (e.g., Bargh et al., 1992; Fazio et al., 1986, 1995). However, other research has employed nouns (i.e., the names of attitude objects) as targets, requiring participants to evaluate the object (e.g., Greenwald et al., 1989, 1996; Hermans et al., 1998). In a similar fashion, Hermans et al. (1994) employed pleasant and unpleasant colour photographs as target stimuli.

Automatic attitude activation also has been found regardless of whether participants are instructed to recite the prime aloud as a "memory word" at the end of each trial (as in Fazio et al., 1986), study the photos presented as primes so as to be able to perform a later detection task (as in Fazio et al., 1995), or provided no specific task to perform with respect to the primes (e.g., Bargh et al., 1992). Although the effect typically emerges on the latencies with which participants indicate their evaluations of the target words, Greenwald and his colleagues have developed a response window procedure that is sensitive to the error rates for evaluatively congruent versus incongruent trials (e.g., Greenwald et al., 1996). Participants are required to respond within a short window of time that begins soon after the presentation of the target. By necessitating fast responding, the procedure substantially increases error rates. However, relatively fewer errors are committed on evaluatively congruent trials.

The affective priming effect also has been found with tasks other than judging the valence of a target. For example, traditional lexical decision tasks have proven sensitive to affective priming (e.g., Hill & Kemp-Wheeler, 1989; Kemp-Wheeler & Hill, 1992; Wittenbrink et al., 1997; but, see Klinger, Burton, & Pitts, 2000). In addition, Sanbonmatsu, Osborne, and Fazio (1986) obtained the effect with a word identification task instead of the adjective connotation task. In this experiment, the target adjective initially was masked by a block of dots which gradually disappeared until the word became legible; participants pressed a key as soon as they were able to identify the word and then recited it aloud. Evaluatively congruent primes produced faster identification than evaluatively incongruent ones did. Finally, the affective priming effect also has been observed with what is referred to as a "naming" or "pronunciation" task in which participants are asked to ignore the prime word and read the target word (typically undegraded) aloud as quickly as possible (e.g., Bargh, Chaiken, Raymond, & Hymes, 1996; Hermans et al., 1994).[2]

Mechanisms mediating the affective priming effect

Fazio et al. (1986) were vague about the specific mechanism responsible for the affective priming effect, alluding only to the spreading of activation in memory from the primed object to the associated evaluation (see p. 231). The activation level of the associated evaluation was presumed to be temporarily enhanced by the presentation of the prime. As a result, less additional activation would be required for the activation of the target adjective to reach the threshold necessary for it to be identified sufficiently that its connotation can be judged.

Unfortunately, the vagueness of this account has led some researchers to the interpretation that Fazio et al. (1986) were suggesting an associative network model in which all positive concepts (be they positive adjectives, positively valued traits, or positively valued objects) were interconnected, as were all negative concepts (see Hermans, De Houwer, & Eelen, this issue; Klauer et al., 1997; Wentura, 1999). For example, Wentura (1999) stated: "Fazio et al. (1986) explained their affective congruency effect as resulting from a spread of activation from the prime to all other concepts with shared valence" (p. 67). This is not a view that Fazio et al. (1986) endorsed. Nor is it required by the logic of their experimental paradigm, for the phenomenon of interest concerned the spread of activation only from the primed object (e.g., "cockroach") to its associated evaluation (e.g., "negative"), not to other concepts or objects that might be of the same valence. As I shall argue shortly, this issue is relevant to the question of mediating mechanism.

Subsequent research has focused much more explicitly on the mechanisms that might be involved in the relatively faster responding affectively congruent prime-target pairs. In particular, several researchers have raised the possibility of an alternative to the spreading activation mechanism, one that involves response competition and/or facilitation (e.g., Hermans, De Houwer, & Eelen, 1996; Klauer, 1998; Klauer et al., 1997; Klinger et al., 2000; Wentura, 1999). The

---

[2] However, various researchers have reported difficulty replicating the affective priming effect with the pronunciation task (De Houwer et al., 1998; De Houwer & Hermans, 1999; Klauer, 1998; Klauer & Musch, 1998). Moreover, recent research by Glaser and Banaji (1999) has revealed a "reverse priming effect" to occur under certain conditions with the pronunciation task. Evaluatively extreme primes resulted in faster pronunciation of evaluatively incongruent targets than of congruent targets, suggestive of an automatic tendency to correct for the biasing influence of the distracting prime that participants were to ignore. Contrary to Bargh et al. (1996), primes that were less polarised with respect to their valence produced null effects. Clearly, the various processes that influence pronunciation latencies are not yet well understood. Nevertheless, the Glaser and Banaji findings do indicate that the evaluations associated with the more extreme primes must have been activated automatically from memory (i.e., prior to the automatic correction process that Glaser and Banaji view as responsible for the reverse priming effect).

essence of the idea is that the attitude activated as a consequence of the prime "readies" the individual to respond in a certain way. If the subsequently presented target is congruent with the prime, responding is facilitated because the response pathway already has received some initiation. On the other hand, if the target is evaluatively incongruent, then the response suggested by the evaluation associated with the prime must be inhibited in order to respond accurately to the target. Thus, the evaluation activated by the prime and that activated by the target either may complement one another and, hence, facilitate responding, or they may conflict with one another and, hence, interfere with responding. This latter possibility corresponds with views regarding the consequences of presenting the word "red" in green ink in the classic Stroop task, prompting researchers to note the parallel between the Stroop effect and the affective priming effect (Klauer, 1998; Klauer et al., 1997; Wentura, 1999).

Importantly, both accounts involve the same initial step. The evaluation associated with the primed object is activated automatically once the prime is presented. Such activation then facilitates the encoding of affectively congruent targets, according to the spreading activation account, or readies an initial response tendency, according to the response competition account. Thus, the difference between the two accounts lies in what follows automatic attitude activation.

Wentura (1999) has provided evidence attesting to the viability of the response competition mechanism. On the basis of literature regarding negative priming, Wentura reasoned that it should be possible to observe evidence that the evaluation associated with a prime is suppressed when the target's valence is incongruent. Any such suppression should slow responding on the subsequent trial in cases where the target valence matches the evaluation that was suppressed on the previous trial. For example, the response competition view maintains that "bad" is suppressed when the prime "death" is followed by the target "wise". Although activated by "death", responding "bad" needs to be suppressed in order to accurately respond that "wise" is "good". If the next trial involves a negatively valenced target (e.g., "lonely"), then the previous suppression of "bad" will hinder accurately indicating that lonely is "bad". Wentura (1999) found evidence of such negative priming, thus confirming that response competition is relevant to the evaluative decision task.

Findings obtained recently by Klinger et al. (2000) also are consistent with the response competition account. Using the response window procedure mentioned earlier, these researchers examined subliminal priming in a task that required participants to evaluate target nouns very quickly. Error rates were higher for trials in which the prime and target were evaluatively incongruent (e.g., "rat/bunny"). However, this affective priming effect did not occur when the participants' task was to indicate whether the target noun was animate or inanimate. In that case, the congruency between the animacy of the prime and the target mattered, but not affective congruency. Thus, congruency with the required response seems to determine the effect of a prime, at least within the response window procedure.

Although I believe that response competition plays a substantial mediating role in the evaluative decision task, I am not convinced that the spreading activation mechanism is irrelevant. In fact, I suspect that both mechanisms contribute to the effects observed in the typical priming paradigm involving the adjective connotation task. As their target words, Fazio et al. (1986) employed adjectives that were purely evaluative in nature, that is, virtually synonymous with *good* (e.g., appealing, delightful, pleasant, enjoyable) or *bad* (e.g., repulsive, disgusting, horrible, offensive). Moreover, the adjectives had little descriptive content and, hence, were potentially applicable to any attitude object. Such adjectives seem very likely to receive some activation as a consequence of their virtually synonymous meaning with the general evaluation that is activated in response to an affectively congruent prime. Hence, they are likely to be encoded more easily following such priming. As a result of the negativity that it automatically activates, the prime "cockroach" is likely to increase the activation level of the target word "disgusting". Indeed, the Sanbonmatsu et al. (1986) findings that were mentioned earlier support such a view. Recall that these researchers employed a degraded word identification task, instead of the adjective connotation task. The target words, which were evaluative adjectives, were more quickly recognised when they were preceded by evaluatively congruent primes. The pronunciation task findings (Bargh et al., 1996; Hermans et al., 1994) also are consistent with the spreading activation account (but, see footnote 2).

As noted earlier, however, other research involving evaluative decision latencies has employed target words that are less directly associated with the primed objects. Adjectives that are clearly irrelevant to the attitude objects (e.g., personality traits such as "wise" or "lonely" paired with physical objects) and even nouns have served as targets. I suspect that the effects in these experiments stem largely from the response competition mechanism.

Obviously, further research is necessary before any firm conclusions can be drawn about the roles of spreading activation and response competition in the evaluative decision paradigm. Such work will need to pay closer attention to the nature of the target words that are employed and to their relation to the primed objects. Because they do not involve the possibility of response competition, degraded word identification and pronunciation tasks may prove fruitful in attempting to discern the manner, and extent to which, spreading activation is involved.

The moderating role of associative strength

One issue regarding the affective priming effect that has proven controversial is the potential moderating role of associative strength. As noted earlier, the Fazio et al. (1986) research was based on a model of attitudes as object-evaluation associations in memory. In addition to demonstrating the automaticity of attitude activation, the experiments were aimed at testing the hypothesis that the strength of the object-evaluation association determines the accessibility of the attitude from memory and, hence, the likelihood that the associated evaluation will be activated automatically upon the individual's exposure to the attitude object. For this reason, the experimental designs included a factor involving primes that could be characterised as having strong versus weak evaluative associations. In the first two experiments, this was accomplished by the selection of primes on an idiosyncratic basis for each and every participant. The very first phase of the experiment involved a task in which participants were asked to make a good/bad judgement for each of a large number of objects as quickly and accurately as possible. The latencies of these responses served as the operational measure of associative strength and, hence, as the basis for idiosyncratic prime selection. Objects for which the participant expressed an attitude most quickly were selected for use as the strong primes, and those for which attitude expression was slowest were selected as weak primes. This strength variable was found to moderate the affective effect. Automatic attitude activation, as indicated by relatively faster responses on evaluatively congruent prime-target trials, was more evident for the strong primes than for the weak primes. In fact, only the strong primes revealed the effect.[3]

Fazio et al.'s third experiment involved a manipulation of associative strength. The primes, which were selected on the basis of normative data, involved objects for which there existed near unanimity about their being positive or negative. A subset of such objects, those for which earlier participants had exhibited the slowest attitude expression latencies, eventually served as the primes. Half of these objects were included in an attitude rehearsal task that participants performed prior to the priming phase of the experiment. Participants expressed their attitudes toward each of these objects multiple times during the course of the task, which was intended to enhance the strength of the object-evaluation association. The remaining objects were presented equally often, but participants simply judged whether these were one-syllable words. Like the idiosyncratic prime selection variable of the earlier experiments, this experimental manipulation of associative strength moderated the automatic activation effect. Although a statistically reliable effect was apparent for the primes assigned to the control task, those for which attitudes had been rehearsed displayed a significantly larger effect. Thus, Fazio et al. (1986) concluded that

---

[3] Subsequent research typically has employed as primes (a) objects toward which individuals express attitudes relatively quickly or (b) objects toward which individuals possess relatively extreme evaluations. Prime selection has been based on either participants' idiosyncratic responses or normative data. Thus, most subsequent research has involved only primes that can be characterised as having relatively strong object-evaluation associations.

the likelihood of automatic attitude activation depends on the strength of the object-evaluation association.

However, this conclusion was challenged by Bargh et al. (1992). They reported a series of experiments in which they observed automatic attitude activation even among primes other than those characterised by relatively strong object-evaluation associations, much like the control condition of Fazio et al.'s third experiment. The ensuing debate involved issues regarding the ability to predict the affective priming effect from normatively based versus idiosyncratically based latency measures of associative strength (Chaiken & Bargh, 1993; Fazio, 1993). In my opinion, the published exchange successfully accomplished two things. First, both parties appear to have agreed that, regardless of whether reliable effects are or are not apparent among ''weak'' primes, the magnitude of any such effect varies as a function of associative strength. Second, the exchange succeeded in clarifying Chaiken and Bargh's (1993) objection to the conclusions drawn by Fazio et al. (1986). Essentially, they (see also Bargh et al., 1996) argued that the moderating effect of associative strength is itself moderated by the extent to which attitudes toward the primes have been considered recently. Both the prime selection phase of Fazio et al.'s (1986) first two experiments and the attitude rehearsal manipulation of their final experiment involved the participants' consideration of attitudes immediately prior to their performance of the priming task. Chaiken and Bargh (1993) suggested that such recent thought temporarily enhances the chronic activation level of evaluations strongly associated with the attitude object more so than it does for the evaluations more weakly associated with the attitude object.

This reasoning prompted Chaiken and Bargh (1993) to conduct an experiment in which a two-day delay was or was not imposed between the initial prime selection phase in which participants reported their attitudes toward a large number of objects and the priming task. The data from the no delay condition replicated the effect observed Fazio et al. (1986)—automatic attitude activation (prime valence × target valence) moderated by attitude strength. In contrast, the attitude activation effect was unmoderated by associative strength in the delay condition. The expected four-way interaction, prime valence × target valence × associative strength × delay, attained a marginal level of statistical significance, $p = .11$. Bargh et al. (1996) extended the argument about the features of the original attitude activation paradigm by proposing that the very nature of adjective connotation task, indicating whether the target adjective means ''good'' or ''bad'', encourages participants to think in terms of evaluation. It was for this reason that they conducted experiments involving the extent to which strong versus weak primes (selected on the basis of normative data) produced evaluatively congruent facilitation in a pronunciation task. Although such facilitation was observed, it was not moderated by associative strength.

As before (Fazio, 1993), I continue to find the Chaiken and Bargh (1993) data puzzling, for both conceptual and empirical reasons. Conceptually, it is not at all clear why recent consideration of one's attitude or an evaluative context should enhance the effects of attitudes involving strongly associated evaluations more than those involving weak associations. The opposite prediction seems just as, if not more, reasonable on any a priori basis. Objects that are weakly associated with an evaluation are ones that individuals typically find difficulty to evaluate. Wouldn't one expect resolution of this difficulty to be more impactful than the simple and quick expression of an evaluative judgement that characterises responses to objects involving strongly associated evaluations? Having decided that "X" is good should promote the development of an association between the expressed valence and the object, and the even temporary enhancement of associative strength should be all the greater for initially weak attitudes than for initially strong ones. Thus, in my view, consideration and expression of a summary evaluation would appear to have a greater effect on what are originally weaker object-evaluation associations. Consistent with this reasoning, Powell and Fazio (1984) found that initial attitude expressions decreased response latencies to an attitudinal inquiry more than did subsequent expressions.

At an empirical level, it is important to recognise that effects of associative strengths have been observed in other research in which a time delay separated an initial experimental phase devoted to the measurement or manipulation of associative strength and the dependent variable. For example, Fazio (1993) summarises an investigation in which the magnitude of the affective priming effect produced by high-resolution colour images of such attitude objects as snakes, puppies, and hot fudge sundae was predicted by individuals' latencies of response to evaluate the attitude objects as assessed three months earlier. Conceptually parallel effects have been observed in research examining the consequences of the strength of object-evaluation associations for attention and categorisation. Moreover, this research did not involve tasks that placed parti- cipants in the evaluative set about which Bargh et al. (1996) were concerned. In work on visual attention. Roskos-Ewoldsen and Fazio (1992) found that objects toward which individuals possessed strongly associated evaluations were more likely to automatically attract attention when presented in the visual field than objects characterised by weaker associations. Importantly, the effect was observed regardless of whether the measurement of associative strength via latency of response to an attitudinal inquiry occurred before or after the attention task. In research examining the categorisation of objects that could be construed in multiple ways (e.g., "Pete Rose" as a "baseball player" or a "gambler"), Smith, Fazio, and Cejka (1996) found that having participants rehearse their attitudes toward one of the two potential categorisations increased the likelihood that the stimulus object would later be categorised accordingly. This effect was observed even when a one-week delay was imposed between the attitude rehearsal manipulation and the categorisation task.

In my view, such effects of the strength of object-evaluation associations are to be expected. Associative strength has been shown to be influential in a large

number of cognitive psychology experiments concerned with semantic priming—experiments using both lexical decision and naming tasks (e.g., de Groot,
Thomassen, & Hudson, 1982; Lorch, 1982; Ratcliff & McCoon, 1981). Associative strength also has proven influential in much social psychological
research concerned with associations other than attitudinal ones (see Fazio,
Williams, & Powell, 2000, for a review). For example, the strength of the
association between the category "charities" and specific members of the
category has been found to influence donation decisions when donors must
generate the potential donees for themselves (Posavac, Sanbonmatsu, & Fazio,
1997). In research concerning the strength of self-associations, Hickfeldt,
Levine, Morgan, and Sprague (1999) found that the latency with which
respondents identified themselves as liberal versus conservative related to the
extent to which participants displayed a consistent ideology in the opinions that
they expressed regarding a variety of social and political issues. Recent research
concerning the direct effects of stereotype activation on behaviour has found that
the extent to which activation of the construct "elderly" diminishes memory
performance depends on how strongly participants' associate the category
"elderly" with the attribute "forgetfulness" (Dijksterhuis, Aarts, Bargh, & van
Knippenberg, in press).

The strength of evaluative associations should be similarly influential. People's general interests and knowledge are bound to affect the extent to which
they form attitudes toward novel objects. For example, some people are very
unaware of national politics, whereas others follow the political scene closely.
The latter are much more likely to develop an evaluative association regarding a
newly emerging figure on the national political scene. Likewise, some people
are avid basketball fans with highly rehearsed attitudes toward teams, players,
and coaches; such individuals also quickly and easily form judgements about
new players and coaches. Others have no evaluation of such basketball-related
attitude objects available in memory, will have little reason to make evaluative
judgements of such entities, and will find doing so difficult if and when the need
arises. Conceptually, such differences in associative strength would appear to
determine the likelihood that a given evaluation is automatically activated when
a given political figure or athlete is presented as a prime.

In addition to the findings already mentioned, some tentative evidence
regarding the importance of associative strength is provided by electrophysiological research. Cacioppo and his colleagues have demonstrated that
when individuals are categorising stimuli evaluatively, a contextual "oddball"
(i.e., a positively valued item in a set of negative context items or a negatively
valued item in a set of positive context items ones) evokes a larger late positive
potential (LPP) of the event-related brain potential (e.g., Cacioppo, Crites,
Bernston, & Coles, 1993; Cacioppo, Crites, Gardner, & Bernston, 1994). In
recent research, Ito and Cacioppo (in press) examined sets of emotionally
evocative pictorial stimuli (e.g., a couple embracing, a chocolate bar, mourners,

at a graveside, and a littered beach) in which the target and context items varied as a function of both positive versus negative evaluation and the presence or absence of people. Of particular interest were the sets involving an evaluative oddball in a condition in which participants were instructed to categorise the stimuli in terms of the presence or absence of people. It is in this case that any evaluative responses to the stimuli are automatic and implicit in nature. Larger LPPs to the evaluative oddballs were observed, even when evaluative categorisation was implicit. Interestingly, such implicit evaluative categorisation effects had not been observed in an earlier experiment that employed the names of foods varying in valence and in status as a vegetable or nonvegetable (Crites & Cacioppo, 1996), suggesting that the effect may be moderated by the extent to which the stimuli themselves are attitude-evoking.

Obviously, more research is necessary, especially work employing the pronunciation task, to achieve a better understanding of the conditions under which strong and weak primes will produce evaluatively congruent facilitation. What may be conceptually most important about the pronunciation paradigm is not so much the absence of an evaluative context, but the fact that any facilitation must involve the spreading activation mechanism discussed earlier and not the response competition mechanism. These two processes may not be equally sensitive in their ability to reveal the automatic activation of strongly versus weakly associated evaluations.

It may prove fruitful to consider modifications to the pronunciation task that might enhance its sensitivity. One possibility that merits investigation is to employ more visually degraded targets. Both the absence of moderating effects of associative strength and the reported failures to replicate the affective priming effect with the pronunciation task (see footnote 2) may stem from the ease of the task and, hence the presence of a ceiling effect on facilitation. Degrading the target words in one way or another may increase the difficulty of the task and provide more opportunity for facilitation effects to emerge. A number of cognitive psychology experiments have directly manipulated stimulus degradation and found this degradation factor to interact with associative strength or relatedness in determining naming latency (e.g., Becker & Killion, 1977; Besner & Smith, 1992; Massaro, Jones, Lipscomb, & Scholz, 1978; Sperber, McCauley, Ragain, & Weil, 1979; Stanovich & West, 1979, 1983). Larger priming effects (i.e., larger effects of associative strength of one kind or another), were observed with more degraded presentations. Some evidence of the relevance of visual degradation to the affective priming effect is provided by De Houwer, Hermans and Spruyt (2000), who recently found a stronger priming effect for evaluatively extreme objects when the target adjectives were degraded than when they were not. In fact, the effect was reliable only in the degraded condition. In a similar fashion, differences between primes that vary in the strength of their evaluative associations may be more apparent in the pronunciation task when the target stimuli are degraded.

It may also prove useful to attend more closely to how the purpose of the primes is described to the participants in the pronunciation paradigm. Typically, participants have not been provided with any justification was to why the primes are being presented and have simply been instructed to ignore them. The "reverse priming effect" observed by Glaser and Banaji (1999), in which evaluatively extreme primes facilitated pronunciation of evaluatively incongruent targets, suggests that this situation can instigate an automatic tendency to correct for the influence of the prime. Such automatic correction processes may have operated to varying degrees in the original Bargh et al. (1996) experiments, the various replication failures (De Houwer et al., 1998; Hermans, 1996; Klauer, 1998; Klauer & Musch, 1998), and the Glaser and Banaji (1999) research as a function of the extent to which the experimental instructions emphasised ignoring the primes and/or provided some justification for their presence. The more participants suspect that the experiment is testing the extent to which they are capable of overcoming any biasing influence of the primes, the more the automatic correction process underlying the "reverse priming effect" may counteract any evaluatively congruent facilitation. It may be interesting to present the primes as "memory words" that need to be recited at the end of each trial (as in the Fazio et al., 1986, experiments) or as stimuli that need to be studied for later recognition in a dual task context (as in the Fazio et al., 1995, work). Providing the participants with a reason for the primes' presence and a task to engage in with respect to the primes may obviate any automatic correction process and increase the likelihood of observing evaluatively congruent facilitation, especially for objects with strongly associated evaluations.

Why automatic attitude activation matters

Unresolved issues regarding the mechanism that mediates the affective priming effect and the moderating role of associative strength should not depreciate the central importance of the phenomena. At a higher order level of analysis, automatic attitude activation is itself a mediating mechanism that plays a role in many significant cognitive and social processes. The extent to which an individual's attitude is capable of automatic activation determines both the power that the attitude exerts on the individual's information processing, judgements, and behaviour and the functional value of possessing the attitude (see Fazio, 1995, 2000, for reviews).

As mentioned earlier, attitude accessibility affects such fundamental processes as attention and categorisation. The research conducted by Roskos-Ewoldsen and Fazio (1992) has demonstrated that attitude accessibility influences visual attention. Objects toward which the participants possessed relatively accessible attitudes, which were termed *attitude-evoking objects*, automatically and inescapably attracted attention. For example, these attitude-evoking objects were: (a) more likely to have been noticed after very brief exposures of each display (experiments 1 and 2), (b) more likely to have been noticed incidentally during a task in which attending to these items was neither required nor optimal (experiment 3) and, (c) more likely to interfere with performance in a visual search task when presented as distractors (experiment 4). It appears that attitudes can be activated from memory at a very early stage in the processing of visual information and that, once activated, such evaluative information directs further attention to the visual stimulus. As a result, attitude-evoking objects are at an advantage in terms of their being consciously noticed and reported. What we "see" appears to be influenced by our possession of accessible attitudes.

Smith et al. (1996) demonstrated a similar effect of attitude accessibility on the categorisation of objects that could be construed in multiple ways. For example, "Pete Rose" was more likely to be categorised as a "baseball player" than as a "gambler" when participants had earlier rehearsed their attitudes toward baseball players; the reverse was true when attitudes toward gamblers had been rehearsed. The findings led Smith et al. (1996) to suggest that the potential categorisations of a target object receive varying degrees of activation on presentation of the object name. However, those categories that automatically evoke attitudes are at an advantage. They attract attention and, other factors being equal, more strongly influence how the target is categorised at that moment in time.

Similarly, Fazio and Dunton (1997) investigated the extent to which perceivers categorised target persons by race. The photographed targets varied in race, gender, and occupation and, hence, could be categorised in multiple ways. In one session, participants were asked to make similarity judgements of all possible pairs of stimulus persons. Automatically activated racial attitudes were assessed a week earlier in a session devoted to a variant of the affective priming paradigm (see Fazio et al., 1995). Faces of Black and White undergraduates served as primes in the standard adjective connotation task. The amount of facilitation on positive versus negative adjectives when those adjectives were preceded by Black faces versus White faces was examined. For each individual participant, the effect size of this interaction between race of photo and valence of adjective served as an estimate of the individual's automatically activated racial attitude. Because the measure is based on evaluations that are automatically activated from memory, the resulting attitude estimates have the advantage of providing an indication of how attitude-evoking race is for any given individual, as well as the valence of this attitude. For some individuals, positivity is automatically evoked in response to the Black faces; for others, negativity is automatically evoked. For other people, neither occurs. Fazio and Dunton (1997) found a curvilinear, U-shaped, relation between the attitude estimates derived from the priming procedure and categorisation by race. Just as in the research on visual attention, those individuals for whom race was attitude-evoking appear to have had their attention automatically drawn to the target's skin colour. As a result, they used race more heavily as a basis for judging similarity.

These various findings illustrate an important influence of accessible attitudes on attention and categorisation—an influence that is itself mediated by the attitude's automatic activation from memory. As a result of their automatic activation early in the processing of information, attitudes orient visual attention and determine how objects are construed. Such effects of accessible attitudes certainly have functional value. The attitudes alert us to the presence of objects that have the potential for hedonic consequences and promote hedonically meaningful categorisations of such objects. We are likely to notice those objects that can provide reward or satisfaction, those that we have personally defined as likeable and can benefit from approaching. Likewise, we are likely to notice those objects toward which we have developed strongly associated negative evaluations, ones that we wish to avoid if at all possible. Recognising its hedonic significance, the individual is now prepared to either approach or avoid the object, whichever is more appropriate given the valence of the activated attitude.

Further evidence regarding the functional value of accessible attitudes as tools for object appraisal is provided by research concerned with the ease of decision making. These experiments employed measures of autonomic reactivity to assess effort expenditure during decision making (Blascovich et al., 1993; Fazio, Blascovich, & Driscoll, 1992). Participants displayed less cardiovascular reactivity when they were deciding between alternatives toward which they already possessed more accessible attitudes. Automatic activation of their attitudes toward the alternatives obviated any need to construct evaluations of the alternatives on the spot, which apparently made the decision task less demanding. Hence, fewer resources were required to cope with the demands of the task.

Attitude activation is a central component in the process by which attitudes guide behaviour. According to the MODE model (Fazio & Towles-Schwen, 1999), automatically activated attitudes can guide behaviour in a relatively spontaneous manner, that is, without the individual's active consideration of the attitude and without the individual's necessary awareness of the influence of the attitude. Instead, the automatically activated attitude will influence how the person construes the object in the immediate situation, and this spontaneous appraisal will affect the person's behavioural response. A prerequisite for this spontaneous attitude-behaviour process, however, is that the attitude be capable of automatic activation.

Recent research employing the priming procedure as a means of assessing automatically activated racial attitudes has revealed relationships between such attitudes and relatively nondeliberative behaviours. For example, Fazio et al. (1995) found that the evaluations automatically activated in response to Black faces were predictive of a Black experimenter's ratings of the friendliness and interest that participants exhibited during a subsequent interaction with her.

Using a conceptually similar priming-based measure of racial attitudes, Dovidio, Kawakami, Johnson, Johnson, and Howard (1997) examined the relation between racial attitudes and nonverbal behaviour that the participants exhibited while interacting with a Black and a White interviewer. The more participants' response latencies during the priming task reflected automatically activated negativity toward Blacks, the more frequently they blinked and the less eye contact they maintained with the Black relative to the White interviewer.

In accord with the MODE model, similar effects of automatically activated racial attitudes have been observed for more deliberative behaviours, but these effects have been moderated by the extent to which individuals report being motivated to control prejudiced reactions. Among individuals with little such motivation, estimates of racial attitudes based on the priming procedure have proven predictive of responses to the Modern Racism Scale and appraisals of the "typical Black male undergraduate" (Dunton & Fazio, 1997). Individuals more motivated to control prejudice displayed evidence of correcting for the influence of any automatically activated negativity toward Blacks.

Instead of directly measuring automatically activated attitudes, other research has measured or manipulated the accessibility of attitudes and found attitude accessibility to moderate the extent to which self-reported attitudes relate to subsequent judgements and behaviour. A variety of field and laboratory research has revealed that such attitude-behaviour consistency is greater for more accessible attitudes (Bassili, 1995, 1996; Fazio, Chen, McDonel, & Sherman, 1982; Fazio, Powell, & Williams, 1989; Fazio & Williams, 1986). In addition, the more accessible the attitude, the more likely it is that new information about the attitude object will be judged in a manner that is congruent with the attitude (Fazio & Williams, 1986; Houston & Fazio, 1989; Schuette & Fazio, 1995). Thus, automatic attitude activation plays a key role in determining the extent which attitudes influence judgements and behaviour.

More extensive reviews of the literature regarding the functional value of acessible attitudes and their effects on information processing, judgement and behaviour can be found elsewhere (see Fazio, 1995, 2000; Fazio & Towles-Schwen, 1999.) The point of this brief overview is simply to illustrate that the automatic activation of any evaluations associated with an attitude object plays a critical role in a number of important phenomena. Attention, categorisation, the ease of decision making, and ultimately, judgements and behaviours themselves are all affected by automatic attitude activation. Attitude development con-stitutes one of the major means by which individuals can structure the multitude of objects, people, and issues that they encounter daily. By forming attitudes, individuals structure their social world into classes of objects that merit either approach or avoidance behaviour (see Allport, 1935; Katz, 1960; Smith, Bruner, & White, 1956). To the extent that these attitudes are readily accessible from memory and, hence, capable of automatic activation from memory when the object is encountered, they provide all the more effective tools for object appraisal and free the individual from some of the impinging demands and stresses of the social environment. Moreover, such automatic attitude activation fosters individuals' approaching objects that have been personally defined as hedonically positive and avoiding those that have been defined as producing negative outcomes. Ultimately, it is for these reasons that concerted effort to understand the specific processes involved in automatic attitude activation and the variables that moderate its occurrence should prove valuable.

This Special Issue

The articles in this Special Issue of *Cognition and Emotion* provide important contributions to our understanding of automatic attitude activation. They relate to many of the issues that I have highlighted in this overview of the literature. In this closing section, I will review some of the essential contributions provided by each article, relating them, whenever possible, to the earlier discussion.

Hermans, De Houwer, and Eelen report three experiments concerned with the temporal characteristics of the affective priming effect. The research relates to previous work that has investigated the duration of the SOA between presentation of the prime and the target. Unlike earlier experiments, however, Hermans et al. examined this variable in a more parametric fashion than has been done in the past, using more SOA levels and, in particular shorter SOAs than typically have been employed. For example, they included an SOA of 0, which involves simultaneous presentation of the prime and target, as well as an SOA of −150, which necessitates presentation of the target prior to the prime. Like past research, Hermans et al. found no evidence of an affective priming effect at longer SOAs; nor was the effect apparent at the SOA of −150. With SOA of 0 and 150, however, participants did indicate the connotation of target adjectives that were evaluatively congruent with the primes more quickly than they did for targets that were evaluatively incongruent. The second experiment displayed similar effects with the pronunciation task. The priming effect was evident at an SOA of 150, but not at an SOA of 1000. These are the first findings to demonstrate the moderating effect of SOA on affective priming in the pronunciation task.

Interestingly, the Hermans et al. studies revealed maximal effects at the SOA of 150, rather than the more typically employed SOA of 300 ms, suggesting that many past experiments might have involved an SOA at which the automatically activated attitude already had begun to dissipate. Of course, the optimally effective SOA may vary as a function of the nature of the prime (words vs. photos), what participants are asked to do with the prime (e.g., remember it for recitation at the end of the trial, study it for a later recognition task, or ignore it), and the extent to which the target is visually degraded. Nevertheless, the findings suggest that priming experiments might benefit from shortening the SOA.

Hermans et al.'s final experiment also offers a novel contribution relevant to the issue of the moderating role of associative strength. Using the adjective connotation task, they observed a relation between the affective priming effect and participants' scores on the Jarvis and Petty (1996) Need to Evaluate Scale. This individual difference measure concerns chronic tendencies to engage in evaluative responding. Jarvis and Petty (1996) documented that individuals with a higher "need to evaluate" were more likely to report having attitudes (i.e., less likely to select a "no opinion" option) toward a variety of social and political issues and also were more likely to provide evaluative thoughts in a free response listing about unfamiliar paintings or about a typical day in their lives. From a large group of students who had been administered the NES in an earlier mass survey, Hermans et al. selected and recruited participants with extemely high or extremely low scores. Whereas the high NES participants displayed the typical affective priming effect, the Low NES did not; in fact, the two groups differed reliably. To my knowledge, this is the first demonstration of a moderating effect of the NES individual difference measure. The finding suggests that there is meaningful variability in the extent to which people experience automatic attitude activation as a function of their chronic tendencies to evaluate objects and form attitudes.

The article by Rothermund, Wentura, and Bak addresses an intriguing question regarding the extent to which attention is automatically directed toward objects that assume differential value as a consequence of the participants' current goals. The experimenters developed a clever paradigm in which two different letters, when presented as target stimuli, signified either an opportunity to gain points if the letter was named quickly (a "chance") or a threat of loss if the letter was named too slowly (a "danger"). Two other letters were neutral in value in that no points could be gained or lost when they were presented as targets. On any given trial, two of the four letters—the chance, the danger, or the two neutral letters—were presented. One letter was displayed in the target light-grey colour; it was this letter that the participant needed to name. Naming latencies for both the chance and the danger stimuli, when they were presented as targets, were faster than for neutral targets. However, a marginally significant asymmetry also was observed; chance targets tended to be named faster than danger targets.

The trials on which chance or danger stimuli were presented, not as targets, but as distractors, are of even greater interest to Rothermund et al. If attention is automatically drawn to stimuli that signal opportunity or threat, then their presence as distractors should interfere with (i.e., slow) the participants' naming of the target letter. Such interference was observed for both chance and danger distractors. In this case, however, the asymmetry was highly reliable. Chance stimuli attracted more attention than did danger stimuli. To my knowledge, this is the first demonstration of an asymmetry in automatic attention attraction in favour of positive stimuli over negative stimuli. The effect stands in contrast to previous findings demonstrating attentional asymmetries in favour of negative stimuli (e.g., Hansen & Hansen, 1988; Pratto & John, 1991) and, hence suggests that the attention-attracting power of positive versus negative stimuli may be context-dependent. In fact, Rothermund et al. found some evidence to this effect. After the introduction of a secondary task that itself concerned the avoidance of a loss, chance stimuli were especially likely to attract more attention than danger stimuli. Thus, when participants were seeking to avoid losses in one task, they were especially sensitive to stimuli that signalled opportunities for gain in the primary task domain. In contrast, when the secondary task concerned potential gains, the asymmetry was eliminated and, in fact, slightly reversed in favour of the danger stimuli.

The article by Musch and Klauer examines affective priming with the more standard evaluative decision task. These researchers emphasise the response competition mechanism discussed earlier and the parallel between affective priming effect in the evaluative decision task and the Stroop effect. Musch and Klauer note that the Stroop effect, despite its automatic basis, has been shown to require that attention be directed to the irrelevant colour word. Narrowing the focus of attention to a single letter in the colour word, for example, attenuates the Stroop effect. Musch and Klauer suggest that the same may be true of the affective priming effect, reasoning which motivated them to manipulate uncertainty about the location of the target word whose valence was to be assessed. Primes and targets (distinguished as such by their font colour) were presented simultaneously (i.e., SOA = 0), in different areas of the screen. In the focused attention condition, a visual cue preceded the word presentation and signaled the location of the target word. In the other condition, the cue always was presented in the center of the screen and, hence, did not narrow attention. As expected, the affective priming effect was reduced, in fact, eliminated, when participants' attention was focused on the location of the target word. Congruency effects also were observed when male and female first names served as the target and distractor words and participants were required to make a decision regarding the gender of the target name.

As Musch and Klauer note, their procedure and findings parallel what has been observed not only with the Stroop task, but also with the flanker task. In recent research that also concerned the latency with which the gender of first names could be decided, Macrae, Bodenhausen, Milne, and Calvini (1999) manipulated the spotlight of attention in a flanker task paradigm. Target words were presented in the centre of the screen and the distracting flankers were simultaneously presented either above or below the target. The visual angle separating the target and flanker was manipulated. Participants were slower to respond to gender-mismatching names than gender-matching ones only with the smaller visual angle. Importantly, Macrae et al. did obtain evidence to indicate that even the more distant flankers were processed. In a subsequent task in which participants were asked to classify items as names of either people or objects, faster latencies were observed for names that had earlier been presented at either the near or far flanker location. Thus, even the distant flankers were processed, but their location outside the spotlight of attention diminished the likelihood that their gender category would be activated. Together, the Musch and Klauer and the Macrae et al. (1999) findings illustrate the important, and obviously functional, value of selective attention mechanisms. Although they clearly receive some processing, not all visual stimuli automatically activate their associated evaluations or categories. Those within the spotlight of attention are afforded a more complete analysis of their associates.

The two articles in the Special Issue that remain to be discussed both employ paradigms that have been developed only recently to study affective associations. De Houwer, Crombez, Baeyens, and Hermans are concerned with the "affective Simon effect"—an affective variant, introduced by De Houwer and Eelen (1998), of the spatial Simon task. The affective Simon task places participants in a particular quandary. Despite the fact that judging valence is irrelevant to their task, participants are asked to use evaluative response alternatives to signal the occurrence of different events. For instance, in the original De Houwer and Eelen (1998) work, participants were instructed to say "positive" whenever a noun appeared and "negative" whenever an adjective appeared (or vide versa). The stimulus words also were evaluatively laden, however. Thus, although the participants' task was to make a grammatical discrimination, the valence of the words was itself related to the response alternatives. If instructed to say "positive" to nouns and stimulus such as "butterfly" was presented, both the fact that a butterfly is positively valued and the fact that it is a noun signal the participants to say "positive". However, if "cockroach" is presented, the signals are crossed; the participants needs to say "positive" because cockroach is a noun, even though cockroach is negatively valued. De Houwer and Elen (1998) found latencies of correct responses to be longer in the latter case of incongruency than in the former case of congruency. In terms of the example, "bufferly" was easier to associate with the response "positive" than was "cockroach".

In the present research, De Houwer et al. demonstrate the generality of the affective Simon effect. Across their first three experiments, both words and photos were employed as stimuli and a variety of different judgemental tasks were examined. The latter included, not only the grammatical judgement employed in the original demonstration, but also categorisation of the stimulus as an animal or person, discrimination on the basis of the stimulus word appearing in upper versus lower case letters, and categorisation of the object depicted in a stimulus photo as either man-made or natural. In all of these variations, stimuli whose associated evaluation matched the valence of the correct judgemental response (i.e., positively valued stimuli for which "positive" was the correct response and negatively valued stimuli for which "negative" was the correct response) were responded to more quickly than those stimuli for which the associated evaluation and the correct response did not match.

The final experiment is an especially clever variation in which motor movement was substituted for the response options of saying "positive" or "negative" aloud. Participants were instructed to press one of two keys to make a computer "manikin" on the screen run towards nouns and away from adjectives (or vice versa). Running towards the stimulus is assumed to reflect the approach behaviour associated with positively valued objects and is the conceptual substitute for the verbal response option "positive". Likewise, running away reflects the escape behaviour typically associated with negatively valued object and constitutes the conceptual analogue to a "negative" verbal response option. Replicating the earlier work, positive stimuli for which the correct response was approach (running towards) and negative stimuli for which the correct response was escape (running away) were responded to more quickly than cases in which the evaluation associated with the stimulus object was incongruent with the required movement.

The article by Swanson, Rudman, and Greenwald also involves a paradigm developed recently to examine affective associations—in this case, the Implicit Association Test (IAT) created by Greenwald, McGhee, and Schwartz (1998). In a manner that is similar to the affective Simon task, the IAT is concerned with the ease with which participants can associate two items. In the affective Simon task, the focus is on the ease with which participants can associate the response option "positive" versus "negative" with the stimulus when the response options are indicative of some dimension other than valence. The IAT focuses on the ease with which participants can associate a response intended to signal a positive (or negative) reaction to the stimulus with a second response regarding some attribute dimension other than evaluation. The critical portion of the IAT involves a combined categorisation task for which a response key has two meanings. For example, in the Swanson et al. research, participants were required to categorise word stimuli as being related to smoking or sweets and as being pleasant or unpleasant. One response key represented both sweets and pleasant, whereas the other key represented both smoking and unpleasant. For a nonsmoker who enjoys sweets, the response mappings are very compatible; sweets are pleasant and smoking is unpleasant. Because any given key has a relatively singular meaning, such a person should be able to respond quite rapidly to the stimuli. However, when the response mappings are reversed, the task proves far more difficult. With smoking and pleasant represented by the same key, and sweets and unpleasant represented by the other key, each key now has dual and, for this individual, incompatible meanings. A comparison of the latencies that the individual exhibits for these two different response mappings provides an indication of the ease with which the individual can associate smoking with pleasant versus sweets with pleasant.

The IAT is intended to serve as an individual difference measure, in the same spirit as recent priming research that has employed lexical decision and evaluative decision latencies to estimate attitudes (e.g., Dovidio et al., 1997; Fazio et al., 1995; Wittenbrink et al., 1997). In the present research, Swanson et al. employ the IAT as an implicit measure of attitudes toward cigarette smoking. Their findings reveal some interesting dissociations between the implicit measure and such direct, explicit measures of attitudes toward smoking as thermometer ratings. For example, although smokers reported more favourable attitudes on the explicit measures, neither of the first two experiments revealed differential IAT scores for smokers and nonsmokers. IAT scores were indicative of negative associations toward smoking even among the smokers. Experiment 3, which employed pictorial stimuli, contrasted scenes that included cigarettes and ashtrays to otherwise identical scenes that did not include these objects. This differs from the contrast between smoking-related items and the items of a distinct category, such as sweets, that was employed in the earlier research. This modification succeeded in enhancing the sensitivity of the IAT to smoking status. Smokers had IAT scores indicative of more favourability toward smoking than did nonsmokers. However, the degree of differentiation was still not as substantial as was true for the thermometer scores.

Interestingly, such dissociation was not observed when vegetarians and omnivores were compared with respect to their scores on implicit and explicit measures of attitudes toward white meat versus nonmeat sources of protein. Swanson et al. suggest that the difference lies in the stigmatised status of smoking and that the relation between implicit and explicit measures is moderated by the degree to which the behaviour is stigmatised. They suggest that smokers' cognitive bolstering of their behaviour is more likely at the conscious, explicit level than at an implicit level.

The future

Clearly, the study of affective associations has enjoyed a substantial boom in recent years. In my view, this special issue represents a significant development in the field's progress. As a result of the intensive research that created the desire for a special issue in the first place and the research reported in the issue itself, we know much more about evaluative associations, their automatic activation from memory, and the various procedures by which such activation can be assessed than could have even been imagined 15–20 years ago. That attitudes can be activated automatically, the very goal of much of the initial research, is now firmly established. We also have learned about various parameters necessary for such activation to be observed. Moreover, such attitude activation can itself have powerful influence on attention, categorisation, judgement, and behaviour. In addition, it is now clear that attitude-evoking stimuli can automatically attract attention, even when they are irrelevant to immediate task concerns, and that asymmetries between positively and negatively valued stimuli in their attention-attraction power can occur.

Despite the obvious progress, many important issues remain to be examined more fully. As noted earlier, further research is needed concerning the potentially multiple mediating mechanisms involved in affective priming. Moreover, more research needs to be conducted with the pronunciation task in order to more fully understand the role of associative strength and the influence of the task that participants are instructed to perform with respect to the prime.

As is evident from the contents of the Special Issue, there has been a proliferation of various techniques by which affective associations can be examined. Not only have various forms of priming tasks been employed (e.g., adjective connotation decisions, evaluative decisions about other objects, and pronunciation), but additional techniques have been developed. The flanker task, the affective Simon task, and the Implicit Association Test have been added to our methodological toolbox. Some of these tasks rely on, and hence, are more suitable for studying, spreading activation mechanisms; others focus on various forms of response competition; and still others are likely to involve both mechanisms. How these various tasks relate to one another and their specific sensitivities clearly will be an important question for future theoretical and empirical work. The issue of interrelations will be especially critical with respect to those tasks that are employed as individual difference measures of attitude.

If the next decade of research is at all comparable to the past decade, considerable progress can be expected in our understanding of the intricacies of evaluative associations. It should prove very exciting.

Manuscript received 21 January 2000
Revised manuscript received 22 February 2000

REFERENCES

Allport, G.W. (1935). Attitudes. In C. Murchison (Eds.), *Handbook of social psychology* (pp. 798–844). Worcester, MA: Clark University Press.

Bargh, J.A., Chaiken, S., Govender, R., & Pratto, F. (1992). The generality of the automatic attitude activation effect. *Journal of Personality and Social Psychology, 62*, 893–912.

Bargh, J.A., Chaiken, S., Raymond, P., & Hymes, C. (1996). The automatic evaluation effect: Unconditional automatic attitude activation with a pronunciation task. *Journal of Experimental Social Psychology, 32*, 104–128.

Bassili, J.N. (1995). Response latency and the accessibility of voting intentions: What contributes to accessibility and how it affects vote choice. *Personality and Social Psychology Bulletin, 21*, 686–695.

Bassili, J.N. (1996). Meta-judgmental versus operative indexes of psychological attributes: The case of measure of attitude strength. *Journal of Personality and Social Psychology, 71*, 637–653.

Becker, C.A., & Killion, T.H. (1977). Interaction of visual and cognitive effects in word recognition. *Journal of Experimental Psychology: Human Perception and Performance, 3*, 389–401.

Besner, D., & Smith, M.C. (1992). Models of visual word recognition: When obscuring the stimulus yields a clearer view. *Journal of Experimental Psychology: Learning, Memory, and Cognition, 18*, 468–482.

Blascovich, J., Ernst, J.M., Tomaka, J., Kelsey, R.M., Salomon, K.L., & Fazio, R.H. (1993). Attitude accessibility as a moderator of autonomic reactivity during decision making. *Journal of Personality and Social Psychology, 64*, 165–176.

Cacioppo, J.T., Crites, S.L. Jr., Bernston, G.G., & Coles, M.G.H. (1993). If attitudes affect how stimuli are processed, should they not affect the event-related brain potential? *Psychological Science, 4*, 108–112.

Cacioppo, J.T., Crites, S.L. Jr., Gardner, W.L., & Bernston, G.G. (1994). Bioelectrical echoes from evaluative categorizations: I. A late positive brain potential that varies as a function of trait negativity and extremity. *Journal of Personality and Social Psychology, 67*, 115–125.

Chaiken, S., & Bargh, J.A. (1993). Occurrence versus moderation of the automatic attitude activation effect. *Journal of Personality and Social Psychology, 64*, 759–765.

Crites, S.L. Jr., & Cacioppo, J.T. (1996). Electrocortical differentiation of evaluative and nonevaluative categorizations. *Psychological Science, 7*, 318–321.

de Groot, A., Thomassen, A., & Hudson, P. (1982). Associative facilitation of word recognition as measured from a neutral prime. *Memory and Cognition, 10*, 358–370.

De Houwer, J., & Eelen, P. (1998). An affective variant of the Simon paradigm. *Cognition and Emotion, 12*, 45–61.

De Houwer, J., & Hermans, D. (1999, June). *Nine attempts to find affective priming of pronunciation responses: Effects of SOA, degradation, and language.* Paper presented at the Tagung der Fachgruppe Sozialpsychologie, Kassel, Germany.

De Houwer, J., Hermans, D., & Eelen, P. (1998). Affective and identity priming with episodically associated stimuli. *Cognition and Emotion, 12*, 145–169.

De Houwer, J., Hermans, D., & Spruyt, A. (2000). *Affective priming of pronuncation responses: Effects of target degradation in Dutch and English.* Unpublished manuscript, University of Southampton, Southampton, UK.

Dijksterhuis, A., Aarts, H., Bargh, J.A., & van Knippenberg, A. (in press). On the relation between associative strength and automatic behavior. *Journal of Experimental Social Psychology.*

Dovidio, J.F., Kawakami, K., Johnson, C., Johnson, B., & Howard, A. (1997). On the nature of prejudice: Automatic and controlled processes. *Journal of Experimental Social Psychology, 33*, 510–540.

Dunton, B.C., & Fazio, R.H. (1997). An individual difference measure of motivation to control prejudiced reactions. *Peronality and Social Psychology Bulletin, 23*, 316–326.

Fazio, R.H. (1993). Variability in the likelihood of automatic attitude activation: Data re-analysis and commentary on Bargh, Chaiken, Govender, and Pratto (1992). *Journal of Personality and Social Psychology, 64*, 753–758, 764–765.

Fazio, R.H. (1995). Attitudes as object-evaluation associations: Determinants, consequences, and correlates of attitude accessibility. In R.E. Petty & J.A. Krosnick (Eds.), *Attitude strength: Antecedents and consequences* (pp. 247–282). Hillsdale, NJ: Erlbaum.

Fazio, R.H. (2000). Accessible attitudes as tools for object appraisal: Their costs and benefits. In G. Maio & J. Olson (Eds.), *Why we evaluate: Functions of attitudes* (pp. 1–36). Mahwah, NJ: Erlbaum.

Fazio, R.H., Blascovich, J., & Driscoll, D.M. (1992). On the functional value of attitudes: The influence of accessible attitudes upon the ease and quality of decision making. *Personality and Social Psychology Bulletin, 18*, 388–401.

Fazio, R.H., Chen, J., McDonel, E.C., & Sherman, S.J. (1982). Attitude accessibility, attitude-behavior consistency, and the strength of the object-evaluation association. *Journal of Experimental Social Psychology, 18*, 339–357.

Fazio, R.H., & Dunton, B.C. (1997). Categorization by race: The impact of automatic and controlled components of racial prejudice. *Journal of Experimental Social Psychology*, *33*, 451–470.

Fazio, R.H., Jackson, J.R., Dunton, B.C., & Williams, C.J. (1995). Variability in automatic activation as an unobtrusive measure of racial attitudes: A bona fide pipeline? *Journal of Personality and Social Psychology*, *69*, 1013–1027.

Fazio, R.H., Powell, M.C., & Williams, C.J. (1989). The role of attitude accessibility in the attitude-to-behaviour process. *Journal of Consumer Research*, *16*, 280–288.

Fazio, R.H., Sanbonmatsu, D.M., Powell, M.C., & Kardes, F.R. (1986). On the automatic activation of attitudes. *Journal of Personality and Social Psychology*, *50*, 229–238.

Fazio, R.H., & Towles-Schwen, T. (1999). The MODE model of attitude-behavior processes. In S. Chaiken & Y. Trope (Eds.), *Dual process theories in social psychology* (pp. 97–116). New York: Guilford.

Fazio, R.H., & Williams, C.J. (1986). Attitude accessibility as a moderator of the attitude-perception and attitude-behavior relations: An investigation of the 1984 presidential election. *Journal of Personality and Social Psychology*, *51*, 505–514.

Fazio, R.H., Williams, C.J., & Powell, M.C. (2000). Measuring associative strength: Category-item associations and their activation from memory. *Political Psychology*, *21*, 7–25.

Giner-Sorolla, R., Garcia, M.T., & Bargh, J.A. (1999). The automatic evaluation of pictures. *Social Cognition*, *17*, 76–96.

Glaser, J., & Banaji, M.R. (1999). When fair is foul and foul is fair: Reverse priming in automatic evaluation. *Journal of Personality and Social Psychology*, *77*, 669–687.

Greenwald, A.G., Draine, S.C., Abrams, R.L. (1996). Three cognitive markers of unconscious semantic activation. *Science*, *273*, 1699–1702.

Greenwald, A.G., Klinger, M.R., & Liu, T.J. (1989). Unconscious processing of dichoptically masked words. *Memory and Cognition*, *17*, 35–47.

Greenwald, A.G., McGhee, D., & Schwartz, J.L.K. (1998). Measuring individual differences in implicit cognition: The implicit association task. *Journal of Personality and Social Psychology*, *74*, 1469–1480.

Hansen, C.F., & Hansen, R.D. (1988). Finding the face in the crowd: An anger superiority effect. *Journal of Personality and Social Psychology*, *54*, 917–924.

Hermans, D. (1996). *Automatische stimulusevaluatie. Een experimentele analyse van de voorwaarden voor evaluatieve stimulusdiscriminatie aan de hand van het affectieve-primingparadigma*. [Automatic stimulus evaluation. An experimental analysis of the preconditions for evaluative stimulus discrimination using an affective priming paradigm]. Unpublished doctoral dissertation. University of Leuven, Belgium.

Hermans, D., De Houwer, J., & Eelen, P. (1994). The affective priming effect: Automatic activation of evaluative information in memory. *Cognition and Emotion*, *8*, 515–533.

Hermans, D., De Houwer, J., & Eelen, P. (1996). Evaluative decision latencies mediated by induced affective sales. *Behaviour Research and Therapy*, *34*, 483–488.

Hermans, D., Baeyens, F., & Eelen, P. (1998). Odours as affective-processing context for word evaluation: A case of cross-modal affective priming. *Cognition and Emotion*, *12*, 601–613.

Hill, A.B., & Kemp-Wheeler, S.M. (1989). The influence of context on lexical decision time for emotional and non-emotional words. *Current Psychology: Research and Reviews*, *8*, 219–227.

Houston, D.A., & Fazio, R.H. (1989). Biased processing as a function of attitude accessibility: Making objective judgments subjectively. *Social Cognition*, *7*, 51–66.

Huckfeldt, R., Levine, J., Morgan, W., & Sprague, J. (1999). Accessibility and the political utility of partisan and ideological orientations. *American Journal of Political Science*, *43*, 888–911.

Ito, T.A., & Cacioppo, J.T. (in press). Electrophysiological evidence of implicit and explicit categorization processes. *Journal of Experimental Social Psychology*.

Jarvis, W.B.G., & Petty, R.E. (1996). The need to evaluate. *Journal of Personality and Social Psychology, 70*, 172–194.

Katz, D. (1960). The functional approach to the study of attitudes. *Public Opinion Quarterly, 24*, 163–204.

Kemp-Wheeler, S.M., & Hill, A.B. (1992). Semantic and emotional priming below objective detection threshold. *Cognition and Emotion, 6*, 113–128.

Klauer, K.C. (1998). Affecting priming. *European Review of Social Psychology, 8*, 63–107.

Klauer, K.C., & Musch, J. (1998, May). *Evidence for no affective priming in the naming task.* Paper presented at the meeting of the American Psychological Society, Washington, DC.

Klauer, K.C., Roßnagel, C., & Musch, J. (1997). List-context effects in evaluative priming. *Journal of Experimental Psychology: Learning, Memory, and Cognition, 23*, 246–255.

Klinger, M.R., Burton, P.C., & Pitts, G.S. (2000). Mechanisms of unconscious priming I: Response competition, not spreading activation. *Journal of Experimental Psychology: Learning, Memory, and Cognition, 26*, 441–455.

Lorch, R.F. Jr. (1982). Priming and search processes in semantic memory: A test of three models of spreading activation. *Journal of Verbal Learning and Verbal Behavior, 21*, 468–492.

Macrae, C.N., Bodenhausen, G.V., Milne, A.B., & Calvini, G. (1999). Seeing more than we can know: Visual attention and category activation. *Journal of Experimental Social Psychology, 35*, 590–602.

Massaro, D.W., Jones, R.D., Lipscomb, D., & Scholz, R. (1978). Role of prior knowledge on naming and lexical decisions with good and poor stimulus information. *Journal of Experimental Psychology: Human Learning and Memory, 4*, 498–512.

Meyer, D.E., & Schvaneveldt, R.W. (1971). Facilitation in recognizing pairs of words. *Journal of Experimental Psychology, 90*, 227–234.

Neely, J.H. (1976). Semantic priming and retrieval from lexical memory: Evidence for facilitatory and inhibitory processes. *Memory and Cognition, 4*, 648–654.

Neely, J.H. (1977). Semantic priming and retrieval from lexical memory: Roles of inhibitionless spreading spreading activation and limited-capacity attention. *Journal of Experimental Psycyology: General, 106*, 225–254.

Posavac, S.S., Sanbonmatsu, D.M., & Fazio, R.H. (1997). Considering the best choice: Effects of salience and accessibility of alternatives on attitude-decision consistency. *Journal of Personality and Social Psychology, 72*, 253–261.

Powell, M.C., & Fazio, R.H. (1984). Attitude accessibility as a function of repeated attitudinal expression. *Personality and Social Psychology Bulletin, 10*, 139–148.

Pratto, F., & John, O.P. (1991). Automatic vigilance: The attention-grabbing power of negative social information. *Journal of Personality and Social Psychology, 61*, 380–391.

Ratcliff, R., & McKoon, G. (1981). Does activation really spread? *Psychological Review, 88*, 454–462.

Roskos-Ewoldsen, D.R., & Fazio, R.H. (1992). On the orienting value of attitudes. Attitude accessibility as a determinant of an object's attraction of visual attention. *Journal of Personality and Social Psychology, 63*, 198–211.

Sanbonmatsu, D.M., Osborne, R.E., & Fazio, R.H. (1986, May). *The measurement of automatic attitude activation.* Paper presented at the meeting of the Midwestern Psychological Association, Chicago.

Schneider, W., & Shiffrin, R.M. (1977). Controlled and automatic human information processing: I. Detection, search, and attention. *Psychological Review, 84*, 1–66.

Schuette, R.A., & Fazio, R.H. (1995). Attitude accessibility and motivation as determinants of biased processing: A test of the MODE model. *Personality and Social Psychology Bulletin, 21*, 704–710.

Shiffrin, R.M. & Schneider, W. (1977). Controlled and automatic human information processing: II. Perceptual learning, automatic attending, and a general theory. *Psychological Review, 84*, 127–190.

Smith, E.R., Fazio, R.H., & Cejka, M.A. (1996). Accessible attitudes influence categorization of multiply categorizable objects. *Journal of Personality and Social Psychology, 71,* 888–898.

Smith, M.B., Bruner, J.S., & White, R.W. (1956). *Opinions and personality.* New York: Wiley.

Sperber, R.D., McCauley, C., Ragain, R.D., & Weil, C.M. (1979). Semantic priming effects on picture and word processing. *Memory and Cognition, 7,* 339–345.

Stanovich, K.E., & West, R.F. (1979). Mechanisms of sentence context effects in reading: Automatic activation and conscious attention. *Memory and Cognition, 7,* 77–85.

Stanovich, K.E., & West, R.F. (1983). On priming by a sentence context. *Journal of Experimental Psychology: General, 112,* 1–36.

Wentura, D. (1999). Activation and inhibition of affective information: Evidence for negative priming in the evaluation task. *Cognition and Emotion, 13,* 65–91.

Wittenbrink, B., Judd, C.M., & Park, B. (1997). Evidence for racial prejudice at the implicit level and its relationship with questionnaire measures. *Journal of Personality and Social Psychology, 72,* 262–274.

COGNITION AND EMOTION, 2001, *15* (2), 143–165

A time course analysis of the affective priming effect

Dirk Hermans

University of Leuven, Belgium

Jan De Houwer

University of Southampton, UK

Paul Eelen

University of Leuven, Belgium

The argument that automatic processes are responsible for affective/evaluative priming effects has been primarily based on studies that have manipulated the stimulus onset asynchrony (SOA; i.e., the interval between the onset of the prime and the onset of the target). Moreover, these SOA studies provide an insight in the time course of the activation processes underlying automatic affect/attitude activation. Based on a fine-grained manipulation of the SOA employing either the evaluative decision task (Experiment 1) and the pronunciation task (Experiment 2) we concluded that affective priming, and hence automatic affect activation, is based on fast-acting automatic processes. The results of Experiment 3 provide a valid explanation for an apparent discrepancy between the results of Experiments 1 and 2 and previous findings. Finally, the results of Experiment 3 support the prediction of Jarvis and Petty (1996) that affective priming effects should be stronger for participants who are more chronically engaged in conscious evaluations.

In a series of priming studies (e.g., Bargh, Chaiken, Govender, & Pratto 1992; Fazio, Sanbonmatsu, Powell, & Kardes, 1986; Hermans, De Houwer, & Eelen, 1994) significant priming effects were demonstrated using prime-target pairs for which the affective relation was manipulated. In affective priming studies, positive or negative prime stimuli (words or pictures) are typically presented for 200 milliseconds and are followed by a positive or negative target stimulus after

Correspondence should be addressed to Dirk Hermans, Department of Psychology, University of Leuven, Tiensestraat 102, B-3000 Leuven, Belgium; e-mail: Dirk.Hermans@psy.kuleuven.ac.be

Dirk Hermans is a postdoctoral researcher at the F.W.O. – Flanders.

We wish to express our gratitude to Frank Baeyens, Geert Crombez, An de Decker, Hilde Hendrickx, Peter Silverans, Anneloes Vandenbroucke, and Deb Vansteenwegen for their valuable contributions for this research and/or for their critical comments on an earlier version of this paper.

http://www.tandf.co.uk/journals/pp/02699931.html   DOI:10.1080/0269993004200033

an interstimulus interval of 100 milliseconds, resulting in a stimulus onset asynchrony of 300 milliseconds (SOA; i.e., the interval between the onset of the prime and the onset of the target). Results show that the time needed to evaluate the target stimuli as either ''positive'' or ''negative'' is significantly shorter when prime and target share the same valence (positive-positive or negative-negative; affectively congruent) as compared to trials on which prime and target are of opposite valence (positive-negative or negative-positive; affectively incongruent).

The generality of this affective priming effect has now been well established by a series of studies. Affective priming effects have been demonstrated for stimuli (attitude objects) as diverse as *words* (Bargh et al., 1992; Chaiken & Bargh, 1993; Fazio et al., 1986; Hermans et al., 1994; Klauer, Rossnagel, & Musch, 1997), *nonsense words* for which an affective meaning was only recently learned (De Houwer, Hermans, & Eelen, 1998a), *simple line drawings* (Giner-Sorolla, Garcia, & Bargh, 1994), *complex real life colour pictures* (Fazio, Jackson, Dunton, & Williams, 1995; Hermans et al., 1994), and *odours* (Hermans, Baeyens, & Eelen, 1998a). Moreover, affective priming effects have been demonstrated using different types of tasks, such as *evaluative categorisation* (e.g., Bargh et al., 1992; Fazio et al., 1986; Hermans et al., 1994; Klauer et al., 1997), *lexical decisions* (Hermans, De Houwer, Smeesters, & Van den Broeck, 1997; Wentura, 1998), and *pronunciation* (Bargh, Chaiken, Raymond, & Hymes, 1996; Hermans et al., 1994).

These data have been taken as evidence for the assumption that human subjects are endowed with an evaluative decision mechanism that allows them to automatically evaluate afferent stimulus information (Hermans & Eelen, 1997; Zajonc, 1980). The idea of automatic stimulus evaluation has been one of the central tenets of several modern cognitive-representational theories of emotion (e.g., Öhman, 1987, 1988; Scherer, 1993), as well as neurophysiological accounts (LeDoux, 1989), and general appraisal models of emotion generation (Lazarus, 1991; Orthony, Clore, & Collins, 1988). Also, several authors within the field of learning psychology (Martin & Levey, 1978), social psychology (Bargh, 1996; Zajonc, 1980) and psychophysiology (Cacioppo, Berntson, & Klein, 1992) have defended the idea of automatic stimulus evaluation.

It is often proposed that the process of automatic stimulus evaluation occurs at a very early stage in information processing, that several stimuli can be evaluated in parallel, and that the basic process is fast, unintentional, efficient, and occurring outside awareness (e.g., Öhman, 1987). In the past, these characteristics have mainly been attributed on the basis of studies that manipulated the SOA level and demonstrated that affective priming effects can be observed at an SOA of 300 ms, but not at a longer SOA of 1000 ms (De Houwer et al., 1998a, experiment 3; Fazio et al., 1986, experiment 2; Hermans *et al.*, 1994, experiment 1). With reference to the studies of Neely (1977) and Posner and Snyder (1975), it has been argued that the short SOA of 300 ms is too brief an interval to permit participants to develop an active expectancy or conscious response strategies, because such conscious and flexible expectancies would require at least 500 ms to develop and to influence responses in priming tasks (Fazio et al., 1986). Hence, if presentation of an attitude object prime influences the response time to a target stimulus, despite an SOA as short as 300 ms, it can only be attributed to an automatic, unintentional activation of the corresponding attitude (Bargh et al., 1992, p. 894). Furthermore, it has been argued that if the priming effects observed at SOA 300 ms were not be based on automatic pro-cesses, but are the product of consciously controlled processes, one would expect stronger or at least similar results if participants are provided with more time to process the prime-target relation. This is because controlled processes are generally assumed to be more time-consuming than automatic processes (Hermans, 1996). Indeed, although in the aforementioned studies (De Houwer et al., 1998a; Fazio et al., 1986; Hermans et al., 1994) affective congruency effects were observed at SOA 300, no effects were present at the longer SOA of 1000 ms. This provides an indirect but rather strong indication of the automatic nature of the attitude/affect activation effect.

However, recent conceptions of automatic and controlled processes (for an overview, see Bargh, 1989, 1992, 1996) have fuelled the idea that it is a precarious enterprise to infer process qualities pertaining to intention, efficiency, and awareness on the basis of these SOA studies. Instead, it is a scientifically more appropriate approach to examine each of these characteristics separately. This has been the goal of a series of recent studies, which have demonstrated that affective priming does not depend on an explicit evaluative goal (*intention characteristic*; Bargh et al., 1996; Hermans et al., 1994), or on the presence of ample processing resources (*efficiency characteristic*; Hermans, Crombez, & Eelen, 2000), and can even be observed for subliminally presented primes (*awareness characteristic*; e.g., Draine & Greenwald, 1998; Greenwald, Klin-ger, & Liu, 1989; Greenwald, Klinger, & Schuh, 1995; Hermans, 1996). Hence, the general conclusion of this research is that affective priming is based on a (relatively) unconditional process, which is automatic in the sense that it is relatively efficient and can occur independent of an evaluative intention and of awareness of the instigating stimulus.

Although the results of the SOA studies should thus not be viewed as a general indicator of automaticity, they are nevertheless interesting because they provide information about the temporal characteristics of the affective priming effect. Based on the results of the aforementioned experiments in which the SOA was manipulated over two levels (SOA 300 and 1000 ms; De Houwer et al., 1998a; Hermans et al., 1994; Fazio et al., 1986), one could argue that the automatic activation of affect is grounded on a fact-acting process. At SOA 300 ms, the level of activation of the associated evaluation was sufficient to facilitate (inhibit) responding to evaluatively congruent (incongruent) targets. At SOA 1000 ms, however, this activation already seems to have dissipated or its influence to be actively suppressed. Presentation of the target at 1000 ms after presentation of the attitude object appears to have been too late for the prime to facilitate responding to affectively congruent target stimuli.

With the series of three experiments presented here, we wanted to corroborate and extend the results of these SOA studies. In Experiment 1, the SOA was manipulated over five short SOA levels to allow for a more detailed view on the time course of the affective priming effect. Also, in Experiment 1, the relative contribution of facilitation and inhibition effects over the different SOA levels was assessed by comparing response latencies for affectively congruent and incongruent prime-target pairs with appropriate neutral control trials. To test whether the observed priming effects for short SOAs can be generalised to other tasks, in Experiment 2, affective priming at short SOAs was investigated using the pronunciation task (Bargh et al., 1996; Hermans et al., 1994). Experiment 3 was devised to test an explanation for the discrepancy between the results of the present Experiments 1 and 2 and prior SOA studies. Finally, and unrelated to our main focus on the effects of SOA manipulations, in Experiment 3 we assessed whether individual differences in engagement in *conscious evaluation* (as measured by the Need to Evaluate Scale; Jarvis & Petty, 1996) would influence the extent of *automatic evaluation* (as measured by the affective priming procedure).

EXPERIMENT 1

The studies that have varied the SOA over 300 ms and 1000 ms only provide a very partial view on the time course of the affective priming effect. Therefore, in Experiment 1, a fine-grained manipulation of the SOA was used to explore this temporal pattern. Given our hypothesis that affective priming effects, and hence automatic affect activation, are based on a fast-acting process, special attention was devoted to the region of short SOAs. More specifically, in the present study the SOA was varied over five different levels: −150 ms, 0 ms, 150 ms, 300 ms, and 450 ms.

Similar research has been reported by Klauer and his co-workers (Klauer et al., 1997, experiment 1). Almost simultaneous with, and independent of our research, they varied the SOA with levels of −100 ms, 0 ms, 100 ms, 200 ms, 600 ms, and 1200 ms, and obtained an affective priming effect for the two shortest non-negative SOAs (SOA 0 ms and SOA 100 ms). However, a crucial difference with the procedure that is typically used in affective priming research is that their proportion of affectively congruent versus affectively congruent trials was 75/25, instead of the standard 50/50 ratio. This uneven proportion has as an important consequence that participants could now use the valence of the prime as a valid predictor of target valence to speed up their evaluative responses. And, although most likely not due to post-lexical or prospective response strategies, this aspect of the procedure indeed has a positive influence on the strength of the priming effect (Klauer et al., 1997, experiment 2). Moreover, this influence seems not to be evenly distributed over the different SOA levels, but is confined to short SOAs. Hence, it is not very obvious to generalise the results from their SOA study to the traditional affective priming paradigm. In one of the between-subjects conditions of a second study, Klauer et al. (1997) did employ the standard 50/50 ratio, but only varied the SOA over three levels, being 0 ms, 200 ms, and 1200 ms. Here, a priming effect was observed for an SOA of 0 ms, which is a first demonstration for affective priming in a standard (supraliminal)[1] affective priming study at an SOA shorter than 300 ms.

In the present study, the standard 50/50 ratio of congruent trials was also used, but the SOA was manipulated over five levels which allowed for a more fine-grained time course analysis under standard conditions. Other differences with Klauer et al. (1997, experiment 2) were that we manipulated the SOA on a within-subjects basis, and that apart from the affectively congruent and incongruent trials, now also control trials were included. These consisted of positive or negative targets that were preceded by individually selected neutral prime words. These control trials will allow for an appropriate baseline to assess the influence of facilitation and inhibition processes in affective priming.

Method

Participants.   A total of 49 first year psychology students (17 men, 32 women) participated for partial fulfilment of course requirements.

Materials.   Targets were 15 positive and 15 negative adjectives selected from Hermans and De Houwer (1994). Positive and negative targets differed significantly on the affective dimension, $t(28) = 46.54$, $p < .0001$ $M_{positive} = 6.21$; $M_{negative} = 1.74$), but not for word length, $t(28) = 0.22$, n.s. ($M_{positive} = 9.0$; $M_{negative} = 8.8$), subjective familiarity, $t(28) = 1.79$, n.s. ($M_{positive} = 5.14$;

---

[1] In *subliminal* affective priming studies very short SOAs are common practice. In our own research (Hermans, 1996), for example, we employed SOAs of 70 and 80 ms. Similarly, Draine and Greenwald (1998) employed SOAs as short as 67 ms. An important dissimilarity with the supraliminal studies discussed here is that the short SOAs in these subliminal studies were mainly obtained by reducing the duration of the presentation of the prime (e.g., 17, 33, or 50 ms in Draine & Greenwald, 1998), which is obviously done to make primes "subliminal". This procedure stands in marked contrast with the short SOAs in the present studies and the research by Klauer et al. (1997), which were not obtained by reducing the presentation duration of the prime, but in which the actual delay between onset of prime and target was varied while keeping prime duration constant (200 ms). Hence it is difficult to compare the data of these subliminal procedures with the data of the latter studies.

$M_{negative}$ = 4.57), or affective extremity, $t(28)$ = 0.53, n.s. ($M_{positive}$ = 2.21; $M_{negative}$ = 2.26).[2] Primes were 10 positive, 10 negative and 10 neutral nouns, selected on an individual basis from a larger set of 119 Dutch nouns (Hermans, 1996). During prime selection, each word was printed on a separate card (9 cm × 13 cm). During the priming phase, primes and targets were presented in white upper-case letters (8 mm high, 5 mm wide) against the black background of an SVGA computer monitor, which was connected to an IBM-compatible 386 computer. A Turbo Pascal 5.0 program operating in SVGA graphics mode controlled presentation of the stimuli. Response times were registered by a voice key that stopped a highly accurate Turbo Pascal timer (Bovens & Brysbaert, 1990) on registration of a sound.

Procedure.   The experiment consisted of three subsequent phases. In the first phase, the *prime selection phase*, participants were handed over the set of 119 words, and were asked to evaluate them on a 21-category scale (−100 = very negative/very unpleasant; 0 = neutral; +100 = very positive/very pleasant). The experimenter stressed that they should rely on their first, spontaneous reaction towards the word. To get an idea about what kinds of words were included in the set, participants took a quick look at the words before starting to rate them.

Following this rating, the participant filled out both parts of the Dutch version of Spielberger's State-Trait Anxiety Inventory (STAI: Spielberger, Gorsuch, Lushene, Vaqy, & Jacobs, 1983; Dutch version [ZBV], Hermans, 1994; Van der Ploeg, Defares, & Spielberger, 1980). This questionnaire was only used as a filler task. Meanwhile, out of the participant's sight, the experimenter selected the ten most positively and the ten most negatively rated words, together with 10 neutral control words. These words were then imported as primes into the computer program.

Next, in the actual *affective priming phase*, participants were told that pairs of words would be presented on the computer screen. They were instructed to attend to the second word and to evaluate it as quickly as possible as either "POSITIVE" or "NEGATIVE", while ignoring the first word (prime), which was only presented to make the task somewhat more difficult. This prime could either precede, follow, or be presented simultaneously with the word they had to evaluate. In order to make it possible for the participant to discriminate prime and target on SOA levels for which there was an overlap in the

---

[2] Affective extremity refers to the (absolute) extent to which the affective rating of a specific word deviates from the mean of the affective rating scale. For example, a word for which the affective score is −2.7 according to the Hermans and De Houwer (1994) norms, has an affective extremity of 1.3 (with "4" as theoretical mean of these 7-point rating scales).

presentation of both stimuli (see below), the target word was always under-scored with a thin white line. Finally, the use of the voice key was explained in detail.

The affective priming phase consisted of 300 experimental trials, subdivided in two series of 150 trials. Within each of both series, there were five blocks of 30 trials for each of the five SOA levels. The presenta-tion order of the five SOA levels was randomised for each participant and for each of the two series of 150 trials separately. In the first half of the priming phase (trials 1–150), each block was preceded by four practice trials, which introduced the SOA that would be used for the following 30 trials. In the second half of the priming phase (trials 151–300), only two practice trials preceded each block.

In each block all 30 primes and 30 targets were presented. For each block, the computer program assigned primes randomly to the targets; the only restriction being that there should be equally large sets of affectively congruent (5 positive-positive, 5 negative-negative), affectively incongruent (5 positive-negative, 5 negative-positive), and control prime-target pairs (5 neutral-positive, 5 neutral-negative). This semi-randomisation was done for each block and each partici-pant separately.

Each trial started with the presentation of a warning tone (200 ms; 1000 Hz), immediately followed by a 500 ms presentation of a fixation cross in the centre of the screen. At the offset of the fixation cross, the prime was presented for 200 ms. Depending on the SOA level, the target was presented before, after, or simultaneous with the prime. For the SOA 450 level, the target followed the offset of the prime after an interstimulus interval (ISI) of 250 ms. The ISI was 100 ms for the SOA 300 level. On trials for which the SOA was 150 ms, the prime was presented alone for 150 ms, followed by a simultaneous presentation of prime and target during 50 ms, after which the prime disappeared. For the SOA 0 level, prime and target appeared simultaneously on the screen, and after 200 ms the prime disappeared. Finally, for the SOA 150 level, the target was presented first during 150 ms, after which the prime also appeared on the screen for 200 ms.

Due to the overlap in the presentation of prime and target for the SOA −150 ms, 0 ms, and 150 ms levels, it was chosen to present both stimuli above one another. This presentation mode was used for each of the five SOA levels. Prime and target were vertically separated about 7 mm from each other (each 3.5 mm from the centre of the screen). For each trial it was determined randomly whether the prime would be presented below or above the target, thus ensuring locational uncertainty of the target (Glaser & Glaser, 1989). The target stayed on the screen until the participant gave a response or 2000 ms elapsed. When the participant had given a correct response, the experimenter entered a code. In case of an incorrect response or in case of a voice key failure a different code was entered. The intertrial interval was always 4 s.

Results

The data from trials on which a voice key failure occurred or on which an incorrect response was given were excluded from the analysis (5.1%), together with all response latencies shorter than 250 ms or longer than 1500 ms (3.87%). The analyses are based on the remaining data (91.03% of all observations).

A priori contrasts were calculated between response latencies for affectively congruent, control, and affectively incongruent trials for each of the SOA levels separately. For the *SOA 450 level*, there was no difference between affectively congruent and affectively incongruent trials ($F = 2.88$; n.s.). Also, none of the comparisons with the control trials was significant, $M_{congruent} = 719$, $M_{control} = 731$, $M_{incongruent} = 734$ (congruent-control: $F = 1.91$, n.s. incongruent-control: $F < 1$). Similarly, for the *SOA 300 level*, the crucial contrast between affectively congruent and incongruent trials failed to reach the conventional level of significance ($F < 1$; $M_{congruent} = 719$, $M_{incongruent} = 728$). Again also none of the comparisons with the control trials ($M_{control} = 716$) was significant ($Fs < 1.21$). For the *SOA 150 level*, however, there was a clear influence of the affective relation between prime and target. Affectively congruent trials led to significantly shorter response latencies than affectively incongruent trials, $F(1, 48) = 13.30$; $p < .001$, $M_{congruent} = 694$, $M_{incongruent} = 724$. With respect to the control trials ($M = 710$) the difference with affectively congruent trials reached significance, $F(1, 48) = 3.44$; $p < .05$, whereas the difference with incongruent trials was only marginally significant, $F(1, 48) = 2.26$; $p = .07$. A similar pattern of results was obtained for the *SOA 0 level*. Here, affectively congruent trials again led to significantly shorter response latencies than affectively incongruent trials, $F(1, 48) = 7.15$; $p < .05$, $M_{congruent} = 818$, $M_{incongruent} = 846$. Control pairs also produced faster response latencies ($M = 813$) than incongruent pairs, $F(1, 48) = 7.49$; $p < .05$, but did not differ from congruent pairs, $F < 1$. Finally, for the *SOA −150 level*, none of the comparisons between congruent, control and incongruent prime-target pairs reached significance ($M_{congruent} = 648$, $M_{control} = 642$, $M_{incongruent} = 642$) (for all three comparisons: $F < 1$).

Discussion

The results show a clear influence of the SOA manipulation.[3] Only for the two shortest, non-negative SOA levels (0 and 150 ms) did we observe a significant effect of affective congruence. This is in line with the idea that the affective priming effect, and hence automatic affect activation, is based on fast-acting

---

[3] In fact, an additional analysis of variance with block (trials 1–150/trials 151–300), SOA (−150/0/150/300/450), target valence (positive/negative), and affective congruence (congruent/incongruent) as within-subjects variables, revealed a main effect of affective congruence, $F(2, 96) = 6.26$; $p < .005$ ($M_{congruent} = 720$, $M_{control} = 723$, $M_{incongruent} = 736$), which was mediated in a significant SOA × Affective Congruence interaction, $F(8, 384) = 2.11$; $p < .05$.

cognitive processes. Although facilitation effects at negative SOAs have been observed in other paradigms (e.g., Kiger & Glass, 1983), no priming effect was found in our study at SOA −150. Most probably, the valence of the prime was not yet fully processed at the moment the participant evaluated the target. Also, when the SOA was prolonged to 300 or 450 ms, significant priming effects were no longer observed. Although this is in line with the idea that affective priming is grounded on quick activation processes that swiftly dissipate, it is still surprising that no significant difference between affectively congruent and affectively incongruent trials was demonstrated at SOA 300. After all, significant priming effects are a standard observation at this SOA level (e.g., Fazio et al., 1986). Nevertheless, in the study by Klauer et al. (1997, experiment 2) there was a similar absence of priming effects at SOA 200 given a significant effect on SOA 0. For the time being we have no valid explanation for this discrepancy, and postpone this discussion until a later moment.

With respect to the proportion of facilitation and inhibition in affective priming, we have to conclude that whereas the congruence effect at SOA 0 is entirely based on inhibition for affectively incongruent trials, facilitation processes seem to have played a more important role in the priming effect at SOA 150. These findings are in line with the results of previous studies which also showed that affective priming effects are due to both facilitation and inhibition (Hermans et al., 1994, experiment 1; Hermans et al., 2000). Although conclusions about the influence of facilitation and inhibition effects are dependent on the appropriateness of the control condition, there are good reasons for assuming that the individually selected neutral prime words that were used as controls in the present experiment provide a suitable basis to assess facilitation and inhibition effects. Hence, theories about the mechanisms that are responsible for the affective priming effect should not only account for inhibition effects, but also for the facilitation effects observed in this and other studies. It would, however, be premature to conclude on the basis of the present findings that these inhibition and facilitation effects would show a different time course.

Experiment 2

To investigate whether the findings of Experiment 1 can be generalised to other response tasks, we originally conducted an exact replication of Experiment 1, but now employing the pronunciation task (Bargh et al., 1996; Hermans et al., 1994). However, in this study (Hermans, 1996, experiment 8), we failed to obtain significant priming effects at each of the five SOA levels. An important aspect of the results was however that the mean response latency in this pronunciation experiment was very short ($M = 376$) as compared to previous affective priming studies which employed the pronunciation task (respectively, 518, 522, and 500 ms for the three studies reported by Bargh et al., 1996; 450 ms in the study reported by Hermans et al., 1994), and as compared to pronunciation studies in general (e.g., Balota & Lorch, 1986, who observed a mean reaction time of 540 ms). One could argue that due to the repeated pronunciation (10 times) of the same set of 30 target words by the participants, the reading/pronunciation process by itself had become so automated that other automatic processes could no longer exert an influence on the speed at which these words were pronounced. Facilitation effects might have simply not shown up because of a floor effect in the response latencies.

For this reason, in the present study, we reduced the number of times the target words had to be pronounced, by reducing the number of (within subjects) SOA levels to three. Also, control primes were no longer used. These changes drastically reduced the number of trials from a total of 300 to 120. The SOAs used in this study were SOA 150, SOA 300, and SOA 1000. The latter SOA was chosen, because until present a discrepancy in priming effects for short and long SOAs, as has repeatedly been demonstrated for the evaluative decision task, has not been investigated in the pronunciation task.

Apart from using the pronunciation task, the reduction of SOA levels, and the omission of control trials, a final difference with Experiment 1 was that primes were no longer selected on an individual basis. In line with previous pronunciation studies, a fixed set of normatively selected primes was now used.

Method

Participants.   A total of 32 second year psychology students (8 men, 24 women) participated for partial fulfilment of course requirements.

Materials.   The selection of primes and targets were based on Hermans and De Houwer (1994). On the basis of their affective and familiarity ratings, 10 positive and 10 negative nouns were selected as primes. They differed significantly for the affective dimension, $t(18) = 20.19, p < .001$ ($M_{positive} = 6.04$; $M_{negative} = 2.01$), but not pertaining to word length, $t(18) = 0.00$, n.s. ($M_{positive} = 5.5$; $M_{negative} = 5.5$), subjective familiarity, $t(18) < 1$, n.s. ($M_{positive} = 5.17$; $M_{negative} = 5.10$), or affective extremity, $t(18) = 0.25$, n.s. ($M_{positive} = 2.04$; $M_{negative} = 1.99$).

Targets were 10 positive and 10 negative adjectives, which differed significantly for the affective dimension, $t(18) = 32.45, p < .001$ ($M_{positive} = 6.04$; $M_{negative} = 1.84$), but not pertaining to word length, $t(18) = 0.31$, n.s. ($M_{positive} = 6.7$; $M_{negative} = 7$), subjective familiarity, $t(18) = 0.473$, n.s. ($M_{positive} = 6.00$; $M_{negative} = 5.88$), or affective extremity, $t(18) = 1.01$, n.s. ($M_{positive} = 2.04$; $M_{negative} = 2.17$). The apparatus and software were the same as in Experiment 1.

Procedure.   The experiment was introduced as a study on word recognition and the speed at which people are able to read words. Because we now used a fixed set of primes, there was no prime selection phase. Instructions for the priming phase were similar to those of Experiment 1, with the exception that no more reference was made to (the importance of) the valence of the stimuli, and that participants were now asked to pronounce the target words.

The experiment consisted of 120 trials, subdivided in two series of 60 trials. Within each of both series, there were three blocks of 20 trials for each of the three SOA levels. The presentation order of these three levels was randomised for each participant, and for each of the two series of 60 trials separately. In the first half of the experiment, four practice trials preceded each block; in the second series of trials, there were only two practice trials for each block.

In each block all 20 primes and targets were presented. The computer program assigned primes randomly to the targets; the only restriction being that there should be equally large sets of affectively congruent (5 positive-positive, 5 negative-negative) and affectively incongruent (5 positive-negative, 5 negative-positive) prime-target pairs. This semi-randomisation was done for each block and each participant separately.

Primes were always presented for 200 ms. For the SOA 300 and the SOA 1000 levels, the interval between the offset of the prime and the onset of the target was 100 ms and 800 ms, respectively. For trials with SOA 150, the target appeared 150 ms after the onset of the prime. The intertrial interval was always 2 s. All other presentation parameters were the same as in Experiment 1, including locational uncertainty at all SOA levels.

Results

The data from trials on which a voice key failure occurred or an incorrect response was given were excluded from the analysis (3.25%), together with all response latencies shorter than 150 ms[4] or longer than 1500 ms (1.75%). The analyses are based on the remaining data (95% of all observations).

As in the previous experiment, a priori contrasts were calculated between congruent and incongruent trials for each of the three levels of the SOA variable. As was predicted, for the *SOA 1000 level*, the difference between affectively congruent and incongruent prime-target pairs proved not to be significant, $F(1,31) < 1$, $M_{congruent} = 413$, $M_{incongruent} = 414$. Also, for the *SOA 300 level* there was no difference between affectively congruent and incongruent trials, $F(1,31) < 1$, $M_{congruent} = 413$, $M_{incongruent} = 414$. At the *SOA 150 level* however, there was a clear effect of affective congruence in the predicted direction, $F(1,31) = 7.21$, $M_{congruent} = 451$, $M_{incongruent} = 465$.

---

[4] In line with previous research (Hermans, 1996), the limits for outliers were set at 150 and 1500 ms instead of 250 and 1500 ms, because mean response latencies for the pronunciation task are significantly shorter as compared to the evaluative decision task.

Discussion

The present results replicate the finding of Experiment 1 that affective priming effects are present at short (SOA 150), but not at longer SOAs (SOA 300, SOA 1000). Also, the priming effect at SOA 150 provides a strong indication for the idea that automatic affect activation is based on processes that are not goal-dependent (Bargh, 1989). In Experiment 2, participants were no longer asked to make conscious evaluations during a prime selection phase or during the priming phase, and no reference was made to the importance of the valence of the stimuli. Therefore, it seems plausible to conclude that an evaluative processing goal (intention characteristic of automaticity) is not a necessary precondition for the automatic affect activation effect to occur.

Although the absence of a priming effect at SOA 1000 and the presence of an effect at SOA 150 confirmed our expectations, the absence of a priming effect at SOA 300 was not predicted given previous results (Bargh et al., 1996; Hermans et al., 1994). One possible explanation relates to the general speed at which target words were pronounced, as was discussed in the introduction to this study. The reduction of the number of times participants had to pronounce the target stimuli indeed seemed to have an effect on the mean pronunciation latency, which was 428 ms in this study, as compared to a mean of 376 ms in the study discussed earlier (Hermans, 1996, experiment 8). Nevertheless, there were marked differences in response latencies between the three SOA levels of the present study. An additional ANOVA with SOA level and congruence as within-subjects variables indeed showed a significant main effect of SOA level, $F(2, 62) = 20.21$; $p < .0001$. Response latencies for the SOA 150 condition ($M = 458$) were significantly longer than response latencies for SOA 300 ($M = 414$) and SOA 1000 ($M = 414$), which did not differ (Tukey HSD a posteriori contrasts). This difference is probably a result of the fact that prime and target are presented simultaneously for some time at SOA 150, which might have been somewhat confusing for the participants. It is possible that the absence of a priming effect at SOA 300 is (partly) due to the relatively short pronunciation latencies, which might again created a floor effect, whereas the longer reaction times at SOA 150 left more room for other processes to have an impact. Without going into the theoretical reasoning behind these observations, we want to point out that a similar positive relation between mean pronunciation latencies and the strength of the priming effect has been described by Williams (1996) for semantic priming tasks. Confirming this idea, we observed significant affective priming in a pronunciation study when responses were retarded by degradation of the target stimulus, but not when targets were undegraded (Hermans et al., 1997). Nevertheless, longer response latencies are not a sufficient precondition to observe affective priming effects in the pronunciation task. Klauer and Musch (1998) for example, obtained similar mean pronunciation latencies as Bargh et al. (1996), but failed to find an effect in a series of experiments.

Another explanation for the absence of priming effects at SOA 300 in Experiments 1 and 2 might however be related to a specific presentation parameter used in these studies. This possibility was investigated in Experiment 3.

EXPERIMENT 3

As discussed before, the absence of affective priming effects at SOA 300 in Experiments 1 and 2 was surprising given the results of previous studies. An important difference between Experiments 1 and 2 and these previous studies on affective priming, however, is that whereas primes and targets are usually presented both on exactly the same place in the centre of the screen, they were now presented one above another, with a distance of approximately 7 mm from each other (each 3.5 mm from the centre of the screen). This physical separation in the presentation of both stimuli was necessary because of the overlap in the presentation of prime and target at the SOA -150 ms, 0 ms, and 150 ms levels. Although locational uncertainty was obtained by changing the position of both stimuli on a random basis, it is however possible that this procedural aspect had a negative influence on the priming effect at SOA 300. Activation effects are indeed known to be sensitive to parametric variables such as the visual angle of presentation (e.g., Holender, 1986). It could be that this parameter has a more detrimental influence on the affective priming effect at SOA 300 than at SOA 150 or SOA 0, if one assumes that SOA 300 is already at the end of the activation curve and priming effects are hence smaller at this level anyway. An indication for the idea that SOA 300 is situated at the edge of the activation curve stems from a series of three studies in which we were unable to replicate the standard affective priming effect in the evaluation task at an SOA of 300 ms, whereas a reduction of the SOA to 150 ms was sufficient for the priming effects to re-emerge in three subsequent studies, all other parameters being equal (Hermans, 1996, experiments 10–15). Also, Greenwald et al. (1995) failed to find priming effects with unmasked primes at SOAs ranging between 250 and 300 ms.

To test the hypothesis that the way in which primes and targets were presented in Experiments 1 and 2 had a detrimental influence on the priming effects at SOA 300, the presentation modus was manipulated in the present experiment. On half of the trials, primes and targets were presented in the traditional way (*centred condition*; i.e., in the centre of the screen), while on the other half, prime and target were presented one above another as was done in Experiments 1 and 2 (*uncentred condition*). As in Experiment 1, the evaluative decision task was employed.

In addition, but unrelated to the previous issue, we wanted to investigate the potential influence on the affective priming effect of inter-individual differences pertaining to a chronic tendency to engage in evaluative responding, also referred to as the need to evaluate (Jarvis & Petty, 1996). Although evaluation is a pervasive and dominant response in judgement for most people across the many situations and objects they encounter, Jarvis and Petty (1996) argued that some people are consistently more prone to engage in evaluation than others. Evidence for this claim was obtained in a series of studies, which were mainly based on the 16-item Need to Evaluate Scale which was specially construed for the purpose of this research, and which has high internal consistency, a single factor structure, high test-retest reliability, and convergent and discriminant validity (Jarvis & Petty, 1996). Based on their findings, these authors proposed some implications for future research. One of them directly touches the issue of automatic attitude/affect activation and affective priming: "Similarly, it would be interesting to examine whether the need to evaluate moderates the likelihood and extent of the automatic attitude activation effect (e.g., Fazio et al., 1986)'' (Jarvis & Petty, 1996, p. 191). To test this hypothesis, two groups of students were invited for the present experiment. One group obtained high scores on the NES (high need to evaluate), while the other group scored low (low need to evaluate). According to their suggestion, a stronger affective priming effect was expected for the high NES group as compared to the low NES group.

Method

Participants.   During the first month of the academic year a group of 384 students filled out the Dutch version (Hermans, 1997) of the Need to Evaluate Scale (NES; Jarvis & Petty, 1996) among five other questionnaires. The mean score for the NES was 52.78 (SD = 10.31), with scores ranging from 27 to 77. Based on their individual score on the NES, 25 students with the highest score, and 25 students with lowest score were invited to participate in this and/or another study (which was unrelated to the present research questions). For the present study, a total of 25 students volunteered to participate. The data of two participants were discarded because of technical problems, together with a third student for whom Dutch was not the mother tongue, and who did not understand all the words. The final sample consisted of 11 participants with a low score on the NES (5 men, 6 women), and 11 participants with a high score on the NES (1 man, 10 women).

Materials.   The stimulus material and the presentation characteristics were exactly the same as in Experiment 2. The experiment was run on an IBM-compatible Pentium computer.

Procedure.   The instructions concerning the evaluative decision task were the same as in Experiment 1. The experiment consisted of 80 experimental trials, subdivided in two series of 40 trials. Each of both series contained one block of 20 trials in which prime and target were presented in the centre of the screen (SOA 300 centred), and one block of 20 trials in which prime and target appeared one above another (SOA 300 uncentred). The order of those two presentation modes (centred vs. uncentred) was determined at random for each series of two blocks, and each participant separately. The presentation parameters and the way in which congruent and incongruent prime-target pairs were construed were the same as for the SOA 300 condition of Experiments 2, with the exception that for the centred condition, the prime and target were both presented on the same location in the centre of the screen.

After the priming phase, the participants were asked whether they had any idea about on the basis of what questionnaire they were invited to participate. None of the participants, however, had any idea. Next, they were asked to fill out the NES for a second time, and finally they were debriefed about the purpose of the study and the selection criteria that were used.

Results

Questionnaire data.   There was a clear significant difference between the high and the low NES groups for the first administration of the NES, on the basis of which they had been selected, and which took place six months before the actual priming experiment, $t(20) = 38.79$, $p < .0001$. The low NES group had a mean score of 33.1 (ranging from 29 to 36), whereas the high NES group had a mean score of 71.2 (ranging from 69 to 75). Although somewhat less strong, there remained a highly significant difference between both groups at the time of testing, $t(20) = 13.83$, $p < .0001$. The low NES group had a mean score of 36.7 (ranging from 30 to 45), whereas the high NES group had a mean score of 65.3 (ranging from 57 to 74).

Response latency data.   The data from trials on which a voice key failure occurred or on which an incorrect response was given were excluded from the analyses (2.84%). In addition, all response latencies shorter than 250 ms or longer than 1500 ms were excluded to reduce the influence of outlier responses (1.14%). The analyses are based on the remaining data (96.02% of all observations).

Conform the results of Experiments 1 and 2, the difference between affectively congruent and affectively incongruent trials was not significant for the uncentred condition, where primes and targets were presented one above another, $F(1, 20) < 1$, n.s., $M_{congruent} = 596$, $M_{incongruent} = 599$. For the centred conditioned there was, however, a significant difference between congruent and incongruent trials in the predicted direction, $F(1, 20) = 3.52$, $p < .05$, $M_{congruent} = 562$, $M_{incongruent} = 578$, thus replicating earlier findings (e.g., Bargh et al., 1992; Fazio et al., 1986).

To investigate the impact of our between-subjects manipulation, an additional analysis of variance was carried out, with group (low NES/high NES) as a between-subjects variable, and block (trials 1–40/trials 41–80), presentation modus (centred/uncentred), target valence (positive/negative), and affective congruence (congruent/incongruent) as within-subjects variables. As predicted by Jarvis and Petty (1996), a significant interaction between group and affective congruence emerged, $F(1, 20) = 4.37$, $p < .05$. Subsequent a priori contrasts showed that the low-NES group did not respond differently to affectively congruent as compared to affectively incongruent trials, $F(1, 20) < 1$, n.s., $M_{congruent} = 584$, $M_{incongruent} = 579$. For the high-NES group on the other hand, this difference was statistically significant, $F(1, 20) = 5.94$, $p < .05$, $M_{congruent} = 574$, $M_{incongruent} = 598$.

Discussion

The results of Experiment 3 lead to two major conclusions. The first is that the absence of the priming effect in the SOA 300 condition of Experiments 1 and 2 is at least partly due to the specific way of presenting prime and target one above another. The fact that this presentation mode had a more detrimental effect on this SOA level than on the shorter SOAs (SOA 150 and SOA 0) is probably due to the fact that SOA 300 is already at the end of the activation curve. Hence, it might be that the priming effects are somewhat underestimated for all of the SOA levels in Experiments 1 and 2 (including SOA 450). Given the presentation overlap at SOAs such as SOA 0 or SOA 150, it is physically impossible to present both prime and target at the same location. But it would be interesting to investigate priming effects at what we expect to be the end of the activation curve of affective priming effects (e.g., SOA 200, SOA 300, SOA 400) using the traditional ''centred'' presentation mode.

Second, a significantly stronger affective priming effect was observed for the high-NES group as compared to the low-NES group. This finding is in line with the proposal of Jarvis and Petty that even though most people might evaluate objects to which they are frequently exposed to an extent that is sufficient to produce automatic activation of that evaluation in memory, the extent of such responding could still reliably vary between individuals (Jarvis & Petty, 1996, p. 173). This difference is attributed to the fact that some people might initially evaluate an object and then seldom if ever engage in evaluation of that object again, whereas, in contrast, other people could retrieve and update their evaluation on a regular basis.

Such an account is reminiscent of a study of Fazio and his co-workers (Fazio et al., 1986, experiment 3) in which participants were asked to consciously evaluate a series of positive and negative words for five times, and for another set of words they had to decide whether or not the word was a one-syllable word. This manipulation had a significant effect on the results of the subsequent affective priming task in which these words were used as primes. For primes that had been repeatedly evaluated prior to the priming phase, the affective priming effect was stronger than for primes for which a nonevaluative decision was asked. This result is easily explained if one assumes that repeated conscious evaluation of an attitude object strengthens the object-evaluation association (Powell & Fazio, 1984), which in turn might facilitate automatic attitude activation.

Similarly, participants that score high on the NES, might possess stronger object-evaluation associations due to their chronic engagement in evaluative responding. It remains, however, somewhat surprising that no affective priming effect at all was observed for the low-NES group, in particular because the primes that were used in Experiment 3 were not unfamiliar, and were rather extremely valenced. Future studies should further examine the role of these individual differences in evaluative responding on affective priming for moderately valenced versus more extremely valenced stimuli.

GENERAL DISCUSSION

The affective priming procedure has become an important tool in the research on automatic evaluative processing. Recent studies that have employed this paradigm have not only demonstrated that automatic stimulus evaluation is a rather general phenomenon which can be generalised to different types of stimuli, but have also established that this automatic activation of evaluations/attitudes is based on processes which are efficient, and can occur independent of an evaluative intention and awareness of the activating stimulus.

The results of the present series of experiments do not only corroborate the conclusions of previous studies which have varied the SOA over two levels (SOA 300 and SOA 1000), but also provide a more detailed analysis of the temporal course of the affective priming effect. Based on the results of Experiments 1 and 2, we can conclude that the activation curve of affective priming has a rather quick onset (SOA 0), with a maximum around SOA 150 after which the effect rather quickly dissipates. Most probably, as is pointed out by the results of Experiment 3, an SOA of 300 ms is already located at the edge of the activation curve. Hence, we can conclude that affective priming shows the signature of fast-acting cognitive processes. At present, it is however still unclear to what extent the decrease in the affective priming effect at larger SOAs is due to a simple diminution of the level of activation, an active process of inhibition, or a combination of both. Together with a more detailed examination of the relative contribution of facilitation and inhibition processes over different SOA levels, the study of the processes involved in the decline of affective priming at longer SOAs, can be regarded as an important future research topic.

The data not only confirm that affective priming effects can be found at very short SOAs using the evaluative decision task (see also Klauer et al., 1997, experiment 2), but the results of Experiment 2 show that this observation can also be generalised to the pronunciation task.

Apart from the fact that the present results provide an insight in the temporal course of affect activation, they are quite consequential with respect to the discussion on the nature of the processes that are responsible for the affective priming effect (see De Houwer, Hermans, Rothermund, & Wentura, 1998b; Hermans, Van den Broeck, & Eelen, 1998b; Klauer, 1998). Based on results with a negative priming variant of the affective priming paradigm, Wentura (1999), for example, has proposed a model for affective priming that is mainly based on response path interference processes. The facilitation effect in the SOA 150 condition is however a strong indication that there is more to affective priming than only such inhibitory processes. Similar facilitation effects were also observed in other studies (Hermans et al., 1994, experiment 1; Hermans et al., 2000). Using individually selected neutral stimuli as control primes, conform the present Experiment 1, Hermans et al. (1994, experiment 1) demonstrated both significant facilitation for affectively congruent trials and significant inhibition for affectively incongruent trials in a picture-picture paradigm (see Hermans, 1996 for the analyses concerning facilitation and inhibition). Because these neutral control primes were selected on an individual basis from the same pool of stimuli as the positive and negative primes, and because we have no reason to believe that these neutral stimuli differed from the negative and positive primes apart from their affective valence, they can be regarded as an appropriate basis to assess facilitation and inhibition effects. This in contrast to other studies (e.g., Fazio et al., 1986) which have employed letter-strings as neutral control primes (e.g., BBB), which not only differ on the evaluative dimension, but also with respect to the ''wordness'' variable. A third strategy for the selection of control primes was adopted in Hermans et al. (2000), who selected prime words on the basis of normative ratings (Hermans & De Houwer, 1994). In this study, neutral control primes only differed with respect to their affective meaning, but not with respect to word length or word familiarity. Nevertheless, again significant facilitation as well as inhibition was observed in the error data, whereas in the response latency data the affective priming effect was only due to facilitation. Taken together, these data strongly suggest that models of affective priming should not only deal with inhibition for affectively incongruent trials, but also have to explain the observed facilitation effects.

With respect to such models of affective priming, De Houwer et al. (1998b) discussed three possible loci of the affective priming effect, which they called the subordinate, superordinate, and response account, respectively. The subordinate account goes back to the original model of Fazio et al. (1986), who proposed a model of affective priming that is similar to the semantic network account of associative priming. Assuming that all concepts with the same valence are linked in semantic memory, activation of the prime concept will spread to concepts with the same valence. As a result, affectively congruent concepts will have a higher activation level than affectively incongruent concepts. Hence, it will take less time for the activation level of the target concept to reach a threshold level that is necessary for identification and subsequent affective categorisation in case of affectively congruent pairs as compared to incongruent prime-target pairs. The essence of the subordinate model is that primes are assumed to facilitate the identification of affectively congruent targets by the pre-activation of subordinate semantic representations of the latter.

Besides priming at a subordinate level, a prime could pre-activate the superordinate semantic representation that corresponds to its valence (i.e., positive or negative). When a prime and target have the same valence, they will activate the same superordinate node. When the valence of the prime and target differ, however, different superordinate nodes will be activated and it will take time in order to solve the conflict. According to this superordinate account, primes bias the decision regarding the valence of the target rather than the decision regarding the identity of the target (as is assumed in subordinate models of affective priming). Besides priming at a super- or subordinate level, De Houwer et al. (1998b) argue that affective priming could also be due to processing at the response level. Assume that participants have to name the valence of the targets by saying "POSITIVE" or "NEGATIVE". In this situation, there are two output nodes representing lexical, phonological, and/or motor information about the two possible responses. After identification of the target, and after the valence of the target has been determined, the correct response node can be activated. One can assume, however, that the prime is also (automatically) processed at these stages and can thus also activate the response node that corresponds to its valence. If this is the case, the response node activated by an incongruent prime will differ from that activated by the target, thus resulting in a response conflict that does not arise when prime and target are affectively congruent. Affective priming is thus attributed to the fact that primes influence a decision regarding the identity of the correct response (De Houwer et al., 1998b). Although the three accounts are explained here with reference to traditional semantic network models, the classification is actually independent of the type of processing model one uses, and can hence easily be translated to, for instance, connectionist models (De Houwer et al., 1998b).

Within the discussion concerning the relative importance of each of these types of processes (De Houwer et al., 1998b; Hermans et al., 1998a; Klauer, 1998), an important role is attributed to the results of a limited series of experiments in which affective priming was demonstrated using a pronunciation task in stead of an evaluation task (e.g., Bargh et al., 1996, experiments 1–3; Hermans et al., 1994, 1997; see also Experiment 2). This is because the results of these pronunciation studies provide relatively strong evidence for the subordinate account, and cannot easily be explained in terms of superordinate or response accounts. For this reason, the pronunciation studies have gained a lot of interest, and it is in this context that the data of Experiment 2 gain additional importance, as they provide extra support for the idea that subordinate processes play a significant role in the production of affective priming effects.

Nevertheless, a number of studies have failed to replicate the affective priming effects in the pronunciation task. As we already noted in the introduction to Experiment 2, we failed to find significant priming effects in a conceptual replication of Experiment 1 using the pronunciation task (Hermans, 1996, experiment 8). Also, Klauer and Musch (1998) failed to replicate the effect in five consecutive experiments, despite using accurate procedures and ensuring sufficient statistical power. Other failures to replicate have been reported by De Houwer et al. (1998a, experiment 2), and Klauer, Rossnagel, and Musch (1995). Hence, doubts have been raised about the robustness of affective priming effects in a pronunciation task. And to make the picture even more complex, Glaser and Banaji (1999) even demonstrated reverse priming effects in a series of five pronunciation studies (i.e., faster responses for incongruent trials as compared to congruent trials).

At the moment, however, we are starting to grasp some of the variables that might be important to understand this complex picture of affective priming results using the pronunciation task (De Houwer & Hermans, 1999; Hermans et al., 1997). And because of its theoretical value with respect to the understanding of the mechanisms behind affective priming, it is our conviction that the study of affective priming effects using the pronunciation task is a line of research that is certainly worth pursuing in the very near future.

Similarly, the results concerning the NES in Experiment 3 open the perspective of a new line of research concerning inter-individual differences in automatic evaluative responding. It will not only be of importance to investigate whether the presently observed interaction between NES and affective congruence can be replicated, but future studies should further examine the role of these individual differences in evaluative responding on affective priming for moderately valenced versus more extremely valenced stimuli.

Manuscript received 3 May 1999
Revised manuscript received 7 November 1999

REFERENCES

Balota, D., & Lorch, R.F. (1986). Depth of automatic spreading activation: Mediated priming effects in pronunciation but not in lexical decisions. *Journal of Experimental Psychology: Learning, Memory, and Cognition, 12,* 336–345.

Bargh, J.A. (1989). Conditional automaticity: Varieties of automatic influence in social perception and cognition. In J.S. Uleman & J.A. Bargh (Eds.), *Unintended thought* (pp. 3–51). New York: Guilford Press.

Bargh, J.A. (1992). The ecology of automaticity: Toward establishing the conditions needed to produce automatic processing effects. *American Journal of Psychology, 105,* 181–199.

Bargh, J.A. (1996). Automaticity in social psychology. In E.T. Higgins & A.W. Kruglanski (Eds.), *Social psychology, Handbook of basic principles* (pp. 169–183). New York: Guilford Press.

Bargh, J.A., Chaiken, S., Govender, R., & Pratto, F. (1992). The generality of the attitude activation effect. *Journal of Personality and Social Psychology, 62,* 893–912.

Bargh, J.A., Chaiken, S., Raymond, P., & Hymes, C. (1996). The automatic evaluation effect: Unconditional automatic attitude activation with a pronunciation task. *Journal of Experimental Social Psychology, 32*, 104–128.

Bovens, N., & Brysbaert, M. (1990). IBM PC/XT/AT and PS/2 Turbo Pascal timing with extended resolution. *Behavior Research Methods, Instruments, and Computers, 22*, 332–334.

Cacioppo, J.T., Berntson, G.G., & Klein, G.G. (1992). What is an emotion? The role of somato-visceral afference with special emphasis on the somatovisceral "illusions". In M.S. Clark (Ed.), *Emotion and Social Psychology*. London: Sage.

Chaiken, S., & Bargh, J.A. (1993). Occurrence versus modification of the automatic activation effect: Reply to Fazio. *Journal of Personality and Social Psychology, 64*, 759–765.

De Houwer, J., & Hermans, D. (1994). Differences in the affective processing of words and pictures. *Cognition and Emotion, 8*, 1–20.

De Houwer, J., & Hermans, D. (1999, June). *Nine attempts to find affective priming of pronunciation responses: Effects of SOA, degradation, and language*. Paper presented at the 7th Tagung der Fachgruppe Sozialpsychologie, Kassel, Germany.

De Houwer, J., Hermans, D., & Eelen, P. (1998a). Affective and identity priming with episodically associated stimuli. *Cognition and Emotion, 12*, 145–169.

De Houwer, J., Hermans, D., Rothermund, K., & Wentura, D. (1998b). *Affective priming of semantic categorization responses: A test of subordinate accounts of affective priming*. Unpublished manuscript.

Draine, S.C., & Greenwald, A.G. (1998). Replicable unconscious semantic priming. *Journal of Experimental Psychology: General, 127*, 286–303.

Fazio, R.H., Jackson, J.R., Dunton, B.C., & Williams, C.J. (1995). Variability in automatic activation as an unobtrusive measure of racial attitudes: A bona fide pipeline? *Journal of Personality and Social Psychology, 69*, 1013–1027.

Fazio, R.H., Sanbonmatsu, D.M., Powell, M.C., & Kardes, F.R. (1986). On the automatic activation of attitudes. *Journal of Personality and Social Psychology, 50*, 229–238.

Giner-Sorolla, R., Garcia, M.T., & Bargh, J.A. (1994). *The automatic evaluation of pictures*. Unpublished manuscript, New York University, New York.

Glaser, J., & Banaji, M.R. (1999). When fair is foul and foul is fair: Reverse priming in automatic evaluation. *Journal of Personality and Social Psychology, 77*, 669–687.

Glaser, W.R., & Glaser, M.O. (1989). Context effects in Stroop-like word and picture processing. *Journal of Experimental Psychology: General, 118*, 13–42.

Greenwald, A.G., Klinger, M.R., & Liu, T.J. (1989). Unconscious processing of dichoptically masked words. *Memory and Cognition, 17*, 35–47.

Greenwald, A.G., Klinger, M.R., & Schuh, E.S. (1995). Activation by marginally perceptible ("subliminal") stimuli: Dissociation of unconscious from conscious cognition. *Journal of Experimental Psychology: General, 124*, 22–42.

Hermans, D. (1994). De Zelf-Beoordelings-Vragenlijst (ZBV) [The State-Trait Anxiety Inventory; Dutch adaptation], *Gedragstherapie, 27*, 145–148.

Hermans, D. (1996). *Automatische stimulusevaluatie. Een experimentele analyse van de voor-waarden voor evaluatieve stimulusdiscriminatie aan de hand van het affectieve primingpar-adigma* [Automatic stimulus evaluation. An experimental analysis of the preconditions for evaluative stimulus discrimination using an affective priming paradigm]. Unpublished doctoral dissertation, University of Leuven, Belgium.

Hermans, D. (1997). *The Need to Evaluate Scale (NES)*. Unpublished authorised Dutch transla-tion.

Hermans, D., Baeyens, F., & Eelen, P. (1998a). Odours as affective processing context for word evaluation: A case of cross-modal affective priming. *Cognition and Emotion, 12*, 601–613.

Hermans, D., Crombez, G., & Eelen, P. (2000). Automatic attitude activation and efficiency: The fourth horseman of automaticity. *Psychologica Belgica, 40*, 3–22.

Hermans, D., & De Houwer, J. (1994). Affective and subjective familiarity ratings of 740 Dutch words. *Psychologica Belgica, 34,* 115–139.

Hermans, D., De Houwer, J., & Eelen, P. (1994). The affective priming effect: Automatic activation of evaluative information in memory. *Cognition and Emotion, 8,* 515–533.

Hermans, D., De Houwer, J., Smeesters, D., & Van den Broeck, A. (1997, June). *Affective priming with associatively unrelated primes and targets.* Paper presented at the 6th Tagung der Fachgruppe Sozialpsychologie, Konstanz, Germany.

Hermans, D., & Eelen, P. (1997). Automatische stimulusevaluatie: experimentele evidentie voor een oude hypothese [Automatic stimulus evaluation: experimental evidence for an old hypothesis]. *Nederlands Tijdschrift voor de Psychologie en haar Grensgebieden, 52,* 57–66.

Hermans, D., Van den Broeck, A., & Eelen, P. (1998b). Affective priming using a colour-naming task: A test of an affective-motivational account of affective priming effects. *Zeitschrift für Experimentelle Psychologie, 45,* 136–148.

Holender, D. (1986). Semantic activation without conscious identification. *Behavioural and Brain Sciences, 9,* 1–66.

Jarvis, W.B.G., & Petty, R.E. (1996). The need to evaluate. *Journal of Personality and Social Psychology, 70,* 172–194.

Kiger, J.I., & Glass, A.L. (1983). The facilitation of lexical decisions by a prime occurring after the target. *Memory & Cognition, 11,* 371–389.

Klauer, K.C. (1998). Affective priming. In W. Stroebe & M. Hewstone (Eds.), *European Review of Social Psychology* (pp. 67–103). New York: Wiley.

Klauer, K.C., & Musch, J. (1998). *Affective priming: The puzzle of the naming task.* Unpublished internal manuscript, University of Bonn, Germany.

Klauer, K.C., Rossnagel, C., & Musch, J. (1995). *Mechanismen affectiven Primings* [Mechanisms of affective priming]. Unpublished internal manuscript, University of Bonn, Germany.

Klauer, K.C., Rossnagel, C., & Musch, J. (1997). List-context effects in evaluative priming. *Journal of Experimental Psychology: Learning, Memory, and Cognition, 23,* 246–255.

Lazarus, R.S. (1991). *Emotion and adaptation.* New York: Oxford University Press.

LeDoux, J.E. (1989). Cognitive-emotional interactions in the brain. *Cognition and Emotion, 3,* 267–289.

Martin, I., & Levey, A.B. (1978). Evaluative conditioning. *Advances in Behaviour Research and Therapy, 1,* 57–102.

Musch, J., & Klauer, K.C. (1997). Der Anteilseffekt beim affektiven Priming: Replikation und Bewertung einer theoretischen Erklärung. *Zeitschrift Für Experimentelle Psychologie, 44,* 266–292.

Neely, J.H. (1977). Semantic priming and retrieval from lexical memory: Roles of inhibitionless spreading activation and limited-capacity attention. *Journal of Experimental Psychology: General, 106,* 226–254.

Öhman, A. (1987). The psychophysiology of emotion: an evolutionary-cognitive perspective. *Advances in Psychophysiology, 2,* 79–127.

Öhman, A. (1988). Preattentive processes in the generation of emotions. In V. Hamilton, G.H. Bower, & N. Frijda (Eds.), *Cognitive perspectives on emotion and motivation.* Dordrecht: Kluwer.

Orthony, A., Clore, G.L., & Collins, A. (1988). *The cognitive structure of emotions.* London: Cambridge University Press.

Posner, M.I., & Snyder, C.R.R. (1975). Facilitation and inhibition in the processing of signals. In P.M.A. Rabbitt & S. Dornic (Eds.), *Attention and performance: V* (pp. 669–682). New York: Academic Press.

Powell, M.C., & Fazio, R.H. (1984). Attitude accessibility as a function of repeated attitudinal expression. *Personality and Social Psychology Bulletin, 10,* 139–148.

Scherer, K.R. (1993). Neuroscience projections to current debates in emotion psychology. *Cognition and Emotion, 7,* 1–42.

Spielberger, C.D., Gorsuch, R.L., Lushene, R., Vagg, P.R., & Jacobs, G.A. (1983). *Manual for the state-trait anxiety inventory*. Palo Alto, CA: Consulting Psychologists Press.

Van der Ploeg, H.M., Defares, P.B., & Spielberger, C.D. (1980). *Handleiding bij de Zelf-Beoordelings Vragenlijst, ZBV* [Manual of the State-Trait Anxiety Inventory; Dutch adaptation]. Lisse: Swets & Zeitlinger.

Wentura, D. (1998). Affectives Priming in der Wortentscheidungsaufgabe: Evidenz für postlexikalische Urteilstendenzen [Affective priming in the lexical decision task: Evidence for postlexical judgmental tendencies]. *Sprache und Kognition, 17*, 125–137.

Wentura, D. (1999). Activation and inhibition of affective information: Evidence for negative priming in the evaluation task. *Cognition and Emotion, 13*, 65–91.

Williams, J.N. (1996). Is automatic priming semantic? *European Journal of Cognitive Psychology, 8*, 113–161.

Zajonc, R.B. (1980). Feeling and thinking. Preferences need no inferences. *American Psychologist, 35*, 151–175.

COGNITION AND EMOTION, 2001, 15 (2), 167–188

Locational uncertainty moderates affective congruency effects in the evaluative decision task

Jochen Musch and Karl Christoph Klauer

Rheinische Friedrich-Wilhelms-Universität Bonn, Germany

Affective congruency effects are often investigated using the evaluative decision task. It was predicted that uncertainty about the location of stimulus presentation moderates the strength of affective congruency effects in this task. In line with this hypothesis, effects of affective congruency were observed in two experiments only if locational uncertainty about the target location required participants to distribute their attention evenly over the visual field. Inducing certainty about the target location allowed participants to narrow their attentional focus and to suppress the influence of irrelevant distractor words. The results suggest that affective congruency effects in the evaluative decision task are not exclusively based on automatic processes, but also depend on a strategic and flexible allocation of attention.

The valence of social stimuli exerts a pervasive effect on social judgements and behaviour. In particular, the evaluation of a first stimulus often affects the processing of subsequent stimuli. In their seminal study of affective priming, Fazio, Sanbonmatsu, Powell, and Kardes (1986) have shown that a target word is classified more easily as positive versus negative if a preceding or simultaneously presented distractor stimulus (the prime) is evaluatively congruent rather than incongruent. Since Fazio et al.'s initial study, affective congruency effects in the evaluative decision task have been replicated numerous times (e.g., Bargh, Chaiken, Govender, & Pratto, 1992; De Houwer, Hermans, & Eelen, 1998a; Greenwald, Draine, & Abrams, 1996; Greenwald, Klinger, & Liu, 1989; Hermans, 1996; Hermans, De Houwer, & Eelen, 1994, 1996; Klauer, Rossnagel, & Musch, 1997; Musch & Klauer, 1997; Wentura, 1999). The focus of the

Correspondence should be addressed to J. Musch at the Psychologisches Institut, University of Bonn, Römerstr. 164, D-53117 Bonn, Germany; e-mail: jochen.musch@uni-bonn.de

The research reported in this paper was supported by grants Kl 614/4-2 and Kl 614/4-3 from the Deutsche Forschungsgemeinschaft to the second author. We are grateful to Ingo Rödiger and the student assistants of the University of Bonn Social and Personality Psychology Department for their help in recruiting participants and in collecting the data.

http://www.tandf.co.uk/journals/pp/02699931.html   DOI:10.1080/0269993004200042

present study is the investigation of a potential moderator of the size of automatic affective congruency effects in the evaluative decision task.

One potential moderator of affective congruency effects that has already been discussed in the original study of Fazio et al. (1986) is the accessibility of the attitude evoked by an attitude object. Fazio et al. (1986) argued that the occurrence of affective congruency effects is limited to strongly valenced stimuli. This claim has caused a considerable debate when Bargh et al. (1992) provided data that demonstrated the occurrence of affective congruency effects even when the affective connotation of the stimuli was not highly accessible. There is as yet no decisive evidence whether high accessibility indeed is a precondition of affective congruency effects in the evaluative decision task (Chaiken & Bargh, 1993; Fazio, 1993).

A second question that has been discussed with respect to the generality of affective congruency effects is that of goal-dependence. Bargh and his co-workers have argued that affective congruency effects are not restricted to situations in which an individuals' goal is to evaluate; rather, according to Bargh, Chaiken, Raymond, and Hymes (1996), affective congruency effects are goal-independent (see also Bargh, 1994). Both in the lexical decision task, in which participants judge whether a target letter string is a word or not (Hill & Kemp-Wheeler, 1989; Wentura, 1998), and in the naming task, in which participants are to pronounce a target word as quickly as possible (Bargh et al., 1996; Hermans, 1996; Hermans et al., 1994), affective congruency effects have been observed. These findings support the notion of goal-independence because both the naming task and the lexical decision task do not require or imply an evaluation of stimuli. Bargh and co-workers (Bargh, 1994; Bargh, 1997; Bargh et al., 1996; Chen & Bargh, 1999) have therefore argued that evaluatively polarised stimuli may produce general and widespread congruency effects even when there is no intention to evaluate any of the stimuli encountered. However, affective congruency effects in the naming task and the lexical decision task tend to be small and could sometimes not be replicated (De Houwer & Hermans, 1999; Franks, Roskos-Ewoldsen, Bilbrey, & Roskos-Ewoldsen, 1998; Glaser & Banaji, 1999; Hermans, 1996; Klauer & Musch, 1998; Klinger, Burton, & Pitts, in press). Moreover, Klauer and Musch (1999) observed strict goal-dependence of affective congruency effects in the evaluative decision task. Affective congruency effects only occurred when the target had to be judged on the evaluative dimension; judgements on physical and syntactic properties of the target were not influenced by the affective congruency of the prime-target pair. De Houwer, Hermans, Rothermund, and Wentura (1998b) did not find evidence for affective congruency effects on judgements of nonevaluative features of stimuli either. Thus, although the available evidence is not yet conclusive, affective congruency effects are firmly and unequivocally established only when the evaluative dimension is task-relevant. Goal-dependency may therefore be an important boundary condition of affective congruency effects (Klauer & Musch, 1999).

Another possible moderator of the occurrence of affective congruency effects that is at the focus of the present study is attention. Bargh (1989, 1994) argued that no allocation of focal attention is necessary to automatically process the evaluative connotation of stimuli, and that evaluative processing occurs unconditionally, on the mere presence of the stimulus in the environment. From a theoretical point of view, this assumption can be challenged. Klauer et al. (1997; Musch & Klauer, 1997) have shown that the proportion of affectively congruent pairs modulates the size of affective congruency effects in the evaluative decision task. They reasoned that this effect is mediated by a strategic allocation of attention to the distracting prime stimulus that takes advantage of the predictive validity of the distractor with respect to the valence of the target (Klauer et al., 1997). They argued that the evaluative decision task can be conceptualised as a selective attention paradigm in which the prime has the function of a distractor. Whether this distractor is being attended to or not seems to depend on whether it provides information that is functional for the judgement of the valence of the target stimulus.

Several researchers have argued that affective congruency effects reflect a response conflict and are thus highly similar to the well-known Stroop effects (De Houwer et al., 1998b; Klauer & Musch, 1999; Klinger et al., 1998; Rothermund & Wentura, 1998; Wentura, 1999). Given this parallel, it is interesting to note that the Stroop effect (often cited as a cornerstone of automaticity; MacLeod, 1991) also depends on attentional factors. An irrelevant colour word produces Stroop interference only when it is attended (Besner & Stolz, 1999; Besner, Stolz, & Boutilier, 1997; Francolini & Egeth, 1980; Gatti & Egeth, 1978; Kahneman & Henik, 1981). If, for example, the focus of spatial attention is narrowed down by precuing a single letter position or by colouring only a single letter in the colour word, the interference of word meaning with the naming of the colour of the word is strongly reduced in magnitude or even eliminated (Besner & Stolz, 1999; Besner, et al., 1997). These and similar findings led us to expect that the effectiveness of primes in affective priming paradigms may well depend on attention being directed to them. The present experiments therefore investigated whether affective congruency effects in the evaluative decision task are moderated by attention.

Locational uncertainty

In a picture-word variant of the Stroop task, Underwood (1976) found locational uncertainty about the two dimensions of the task to be influential. When participants knew where to expect the relevant picture and the spatially separated irrelevant word, they showed only a small amount of interference from the competing word when naming the picture. When they did not know where to expect the two stimuli, interference was considerably greater. Obviously, under locational uncertainty, participants were not able to focus their attention and had to accept more information from the irrelevant word. In a similar vein, Kahneman, Treisman, and Burkell (1983) and Kahneman and Treisman (1984) required their participants to focus attention on word stimuli that could be distinguished from distractors on the basis of simple visual features. When target location was uncertain, and when a naming response was required, performance was impaired by concurrent presentation of distractors, and the amount of impairment was proportional to the number of distractors presented. However, if a precue informed participants of target location, the adverse effect of distractor presentation was minimised. In the so-called flanker task (Eriksen & Eriksen, 1974; Eriksen & Shultz, 1979), positional uncertainty also has a large effect on the magnitude of the effects of irrelevant flankers. Interference effects are greatly attenuated when attention is predirected to the place where the target is about to appear (Paquet & Lortie, 1990; Yantis & Johnston, 1990).

Theoretically, the effects of locational uncertainty can be understood on the basis of theories of selective attention. Based on a thorough review of the experimental literature on selective attention, Johnston and Dark (1986) concluded that the deployment of attention in the visual space can be likened to the operation of a beam of a "spotlight" (Posner, Snyder, & Davidson, 1980). The beam is characterised by a specific size, which can vary according to task demands (LaBerge, 1983; Umilta, 1988). Under certain conditions, such as locational uncertainty about the target location, the resources of the attentional system are distributed evenly over the entire display, with parallel processing of the display items. The beam of attention has a "wide setting" (LaBerge, 1983) in this distributed-attention condition. In contrast, if the target location is known in advance, the beam of attention has a narrow setting and is concentrated on only one display location (Duncan, 1980; Jonides, 1983). Focusing attention accomplishes an important goal: allowing to-be-attended objects to be processed without interference from to-be ignored objects. A narrow setting of the attentional beam can be induced by presenting visual precues which elicit fast, automatic shifts of attention toward the precued location of the target stimulus, establishing an optimal focused-attention condition (Johnston & Dark, 1986; Müller & Rabbitt, 1989).[1]

---

[1] Distributed and focused attention are not necessarily two dichotomous modes of processing. Eriksen and Yeh (1985) have argued that the two conditions may merely be poles on a continuum of attentional distribution ranging from concentration on a single, small area to a uniform spread of attention over the entire visual field. The present experiments aim at contrasting the two extremes of the proposed continuum, however, and it is not important for this purpose to decide whether the dichotomous model or the continuous model is more appropriate. The spotlight metaphor has also recently been challenged by proponents of an activity-distribution model (LaBerge, Carlson, Williams, & Bunney, 1997). However, the present reasoning can be upheld regardless of whether attention is conceptualised as preparatory attentional activity that can be concentrated on a single area as well as distributed evenly across the visual field, or whether attention is seen as a moving spotlight of varying size.

EXPERIMENT 1

If affective congruency effects are moderated by attention, a manipulation of locational uncertainty to induce distributed versus focused attention should have similar effects in the evaluative decision task as in spatially separated Stroop variants and flanker tasks. The hypothesis for Experiment 1 therefore was that affective congruency effects by spatially separated distractor stimuli would be sharply curtailed if attention was predirected to the target location. If affective congruency effects are linked to inefficient selection of the target, prior knowledge of its precise location may prevent spreading of attention to the prime. According to this argument, early target selection based on spatial location would facilitate exclusion of the valence of the distractor from processing, and consequently, affective congruency effects should be strongly reduced. If a reduction in the size of the effect can indeed be found, this would have severe consequences for the notion that affective congruency effects are unconditional in nature.

In the experiment, target words were presented at random locations on the screen. Uncertainty about the target location was varied between subjects by either presenting a precue at the location of the upcoming target (focused-attention condition), or by presenting an uninformative, neutral cue in the centre of the display which had no predictive value regarding the position of the upcoming target (distributed-attention condition). Based on similar findings in selective attention paradigms, a moderating effect of locational uncertainty on the magnitude of affective congruency effects was predicted. Stronger effects were expected in the distributed-attention condition than in the focused-attention condition.

Affective congruency effects may involve the operation of a separate affective processing system that operates by different rules than does non-affective cognitive processing (Bargh, 1997; Hermans, van den Broeck, & Eelen, 1998; Murphy & Zajonc , 1993; Zajonc, 1980). To assess this possibility, each participant dealt with a second task in addition to the evaluative decision task in which the evaluatively polarised words were replaced by male and female first names and a decision on the gender of the target name was required. The first-names material provides a strong control condition because it is closely parallel to evaluatively polarised material in a number of respects. In the gender decision task, as in the evaluative decision task, large categories of words are mapped onto two mutually exclusive response categories. Furthermore, like evaluations, gender appears to be activated and encoded spontaneously (Taylor, Fiske, Etcoff, & Ruderman, 1978). Importantly, a number of researchers have used first names and the gender decision task and have found congruency effects analogous to the ones found in the evaluative decision task (e.g., Blair & Banaji, 1996; Greenwald et al., 1996; Macrae, Bodenhausen, Milne, Thorn, & Castelli, 1997). When the two names are consistent rather than inconsistent in their gender implications, gender decisions on the target are facilitated. As in affective priming, subliminal effects occur (Draine & Greenwald, 1998), and there are consistency proportion effects (Blair & Banaji, 1996) even with short SOAs. To the extent to which effects of locational uncertainty obtained with evaluatively polarised stimuli parallel the effects obtained with the first-names material, a special role of the affective dimension need not be postulated.

Method

Participants.   These were 32 University of Bonn students from different faculties and nonstudent volunteers of a similar age range recruited by the experimenters. Psychology students received partial course credit. Students from other faculties were paid DM 10 (approx. US $6) for their participation, and nonstudent volunteers participated in exchange for detailed individual feedback on their results. All participants were native speaker of German and had normal or corrected-to-normal vision.

Procedure.   Each participant was tested individually and performed both evaluative decisions on the polarised adjectives and gender decisions on the first names. The order in which the two tasks had to be performed was counterbalanced across participants. Stimuli were presented in the middle of a 17-inch VGA colour monitor. Stimulus presentation and measurement of response latencies utilised a software timer and video synchronisation by Haussmann (1992).

Participants were seated at a distance of 50 cm in front of the computer screen. The background colour of the screen was light grey. Uncertainty about the target location in each trial was varied between subjects by presenting a precue at the location of the upcoming target to half of the participants (focused-attention condition), and by presenting a neutral cue in the centre of the display to the other half of participants (distributed-attention condition). In both conditions, the cue consisted of the letter "X".

For both the focused-attention and the divided-attention group, onset of the precue preceded onset of the distractor stimulus and the target (which were presented simultaneously) by 600 ms. As demonstrated by Butler (1974), a peripheral precue preceding a display by this length of time is sufficient to induce visual selective attention. A neutral (central) cue instead of no cue was used in the distributed-attention condition because neutral cues produce the same general alerting effects as valid cues (Logan & Zbrodoff, 1982; Posner & Boies, 1971), but do not provide information that would allow participants to attend selectively to the target stimulus. The precue disappeared 300 ms prior to the onset of the distractor and the target. Different colours were chosen for the distractors and the targets to enable discrimination of the to-be-attended items from the to-be-ignored items. The distractors were presented in red for 200 ms.

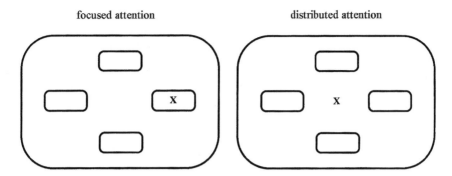

Figure 1. Manipulating locational uncertainty by presenting visual precues at the location of the upcoming target (focused-attention condition) or in the centre of the display (distributed-attention condition).

The target words were presented simultaneously (SOA 0 ms) in black. Distractor and target stimuli were presented at one of four possible places which were located at a distance of 7 cm above, below, to the left or to the right of the centre of the screen. The positions of both distractor and target were randomly determined for each trial with the restriction that distractor and target were not presented at the same place. The four possible stimulus locations are visualised by rectangles (which were not presented during the experiment) in Figure 1.

Material.   First names. From a large list of common German first names (Voorgang, 1994), 208 male and 192 female names were selected. In a pilot study, 40 psychology students (22 female, 18 male) receiving partial course credit or small monetary compensation rated each of the 208 male and 192 female names with respect to how commonly they were used in ordinary German. In addition they classified all name with respect to gender (male vs. female) in a speeded binary forced-choice task. For each name: (1) the average rating of familiarity, (2) the average speed, and (3) the consistency of the gender decision was computed across participants. These three measures were *z*-standardised and entered, with equal weights, into a single composite index on the basis of which 70 typical and easy-to-recognise male, and 70 typical and easy-to-recognise female names were then selected. In doing so, an additional constraint was that only names with a length of three to eight letters were eligible. The resulting sets of names were already used successfully in a previous study on affective congruency effects (Klauer & Musch, 1999).

Adjectives. German adjectives that were strongly polarised in valence were used as distractors and targets in all experiments. We selected 70 strongly positive and 70 strongly negative adjectives from a pool of polarised adjectives used in previous affective priming experiments (e.g., Klauer et al., 1997) with the restriction that each word had between three and nine letters. A higher maximum of letters had to be allowed than for the first-names material (nine rather than eight) to obtain the desired large number of suitable adjectives.

List construction.   For each participant, a new list of distractor-target pairs was constructed. Each participant's list consisted of blocks of 48 distractor-target pairs (and at least five practice blocks of 36 distractor-target pairs constructed analogously). Blocks were based on the evaluatively polarised material in one phase of the experiment and on the first-names material in the other. For each block, all stimuli were randomly sampled without replacement from the pools of 70 positive and 70 negative adjectives (from the pools of 70 male and 70 female names). Thus, any given word or name occurred at most once in a given block.

On one-third of the trials in the practice and experimental blocks, congruent distractor-target pairs (i.e., words of the same valence or names of the same gender) were used. Half of the congruent pairs consisted of two positive (two male) stimuli, the other half of the congruent pairs consisted of two negative (two female) stimuli. Another third of the trials consisted of incongruent distractor-target pairs (i.e., words of opposite valence or names of different gender). Half of the incongruent pairs consisted of a positive and a negative word (a male and a female name), the other half consisted of a negative and a positive word (a female and a male name). One-half of the last third of trials contained positive (male) and one half contained negative (female) targets. The targets in this last third of trials were accompanied by neutral distractors consisting of meaningless letter strings which corresponded in length to the mean length of the adjectives (names) used. The meaningless letter strings were assembled from letters that were drawn randomly from the alphabet (excluding the letters a, e, i, o, u, q, x, y, z to avoid creating stimuli that resemble real words or that contain a high number of rare letters). In the evaluative decision task, the neutral distractors were presented in lower case (e.g., "bnvwthm") to resemble the adjectives used (e.g., "ehrlich"—*honest*) most closely. In the gender decision task, the neutral distractors were presented in lower case with the exception of the first letter, which was presented in upper case (e.g., "Mrwpsb") to resemble the first names (e.g., "Martin") as closely as possible. Congruent, incongruent, and neutral trials were presented in randomised order in each block.

Response key assignments.   Both in the evaluative decision task and in the gender decision task, participants were asked to indicate their decision by pressing one of two response keys. The response keys were the "space" key of a standard computer keyboard to be pressed with left hand and the "enter" key on the right-side numeric keypad to be pressed with the right hand. The assignment of response keys to the response alternatives was counterbalanced across participants within each task.

Response window procedure.   The response window procedure proposed by Greenwald et al. (1996) was employed to push participants toward responding within a narrow time frame after the presentation of the target. As Greenwald et al. (1996) have pointed out, this technique has the major benefit of controlling for speed-accuracy trade-off problems by forcing all response latencies to be relatively similar, thereby avoiding the dilution of possible effects amongst both response latency and accuracy. The dependent variable with this procedure is the percentage of correct responses (Draine & Greenwald, 1998; Klauer & Musch, 1999; Klinger et al., in press).

Participants had a window of 133 ms duration within which they were to respond to the target item. The centre of this window was initially at 400 ms after target presentation. Thus, at the outset of the experiment the response window began 333 ms after target onset, giving participants the interval between 333 ms and 467 ms after target presentation to respond. To tailor the window centre to each participant's performance and to adapt to changes in performance accuracy over the course of the experiment, an adaptive procedure modelled closely after Draine and Greenwald (1998) was used. As detailed later, the window centre was adjusted contingent on the participant's accuracy. This ensured that both floor and ceiling effects in the overall error rates on each task were avoided.

Participants were informed that all responses after the response window were too slow and that they should try to enter all of their responses during the response window. Window onset was signalled by a change in colour of the target word from black to yellow. Feedback for success was provided by the target's behaviour. If the response occurred before onset of the response window, the target never changed to yellow. If the response was not too early, the target changed to yellow 333 ms after target onset, marking the beginning of the 133 ms response window. If the response occurred during the window, the target word changed from yellow to white and remained white for 300 ms. The screen was then cleared and the next trial was initiated after an additional 400 ms had passed. If no response was made during the response window, the target word changed black again for 300 ms after the end of the response window. The screen was then cleared, and the next trial was initiated after an additional 400 ms interval.

In all experiments, the adaptive response window was initially centred at 400 ms after onset of the target word. At the end of each block, the window centre could decrease by 33 ms, increase by 33 ms, or could remain unchanged, depending on the participant's performance in that block. Following Draine and Greenwald (1998), the window centre was made shorter if the error percentage was less than or equal to 20% *and* the participant's mean response latency for that block did not exceed the current window by more than 100 ms. The window centre was made longer if the participant's error percentage was greater than or equal to 45% *and* the mean response latency exceeded the current window centre by more than 100 ms. If neither of these sets of conditions was met, the window centre was not changed. Only trials in which the participant responded in the interval between 100 ms and 1000 ms after target onset were included in determining percentage correct scores.

Practice and experimental blocks. Participants completed five to twelve blocks of practice trials prior to the experimental trials for each kind of material (adjectives vs. names, respectively). During the first two blocks of 36 practice trials each, no distractor stimuli were displayed (blank fields were presented in their place), and the response window was not used. Participants were free to respond however quickly or slowly they desired in order to practise their task. They were given feedback at the end of each trial as to whether they entered the correct response or not.

The following blocks of 36 practice trials added the response window to the procedures of the first two practice blocks. At the beginning of each practice and experimental block with the response window, six additional dummy trials consisting of the same kind of stimulus pairs were presented. Participants were instructed to observe these trials without giving a response so that they could adjust to the temporal placement of the response window. The start of the 36 practice trials in each block was indicated by a beep of the computer's internal speaker.

Participants had to perform a minimum of three practice blocks with response windows prior to each of the two phases of experimental blocks in the experiment. They continued practising until no further adaptation of the window centre was necessary or until a maximum number of ten practice blocks using the response window was reached. For each kind of material (adjectives vs. names), following the practice trials, participants completed six blocks of 48 experimental trials each. Thus, for both adjectives and names, analyses were performed on $6 \times 48 = 288$ experimental trials. After each practice and experimental block, participants were informed of their percentage of correct responses and were advised that, although relatively high error rates could normally occur, they should nevertheless try to respond as accurately as possible. Participants were allowed to rest briefly between each practice and experimental block. The sessions of each experiment lasted about 45 minutes.

Results

Of main interest is the dependency of the congruency effect from locational uncertainty. Therefore, congruency effects in the evaluative decision task and the gender decision task were computed by subtracting percentage correct for trials with incongruent word pairs from percentage correct for trials with

TABLE 1

Percentage errors and congruency effects (and their standard deviations) in Experiment 1 as a function of the kind of material, locational uncertainty, and kind of pair

Material	Location	Kind of pair			Congruency effect
		Congruent	Neutral	Incongruent	
Adjectives	Uncertain	37.1 (11.3)	38.9 (10.5)	42.5 (9.9)	5.4 (5.7)
	Certain	29.4 (7.9)	28.6 (7.9)	28.6 (9.1)	−0.8 (8.3)
Names	Uncertain	33.2 (10.8)	33.4 (9.1)	38.1 (9.1)	4.9 (6.5)
	Certain	24.6 (7.5)	25.1 (5.3)	24.2 (7.1)	−0.4 (7.1)

Note: Congruency effects were computed as the percentage errors difference between incongruent and congruent pairs.

congruent pairs. Table 1 shows the congruency effects in both tasks as a function of locational uncertainty.

An analysis of variance with the within-subjects factor "task" (evaluative decision on adjectives vs. gender decision on names) and the between-subjects factor "locational uncertainty" was performed on the congruency effects. There was a significant effect of locational uncertainty, $F(1, 30) = 8.26$, $p < .01$, but no effect of task (evaluative decision vs. gender decision), $F(1, 30) = 0.02$. The interaction of task and locational uncertainty was not significant, $F(1, 30) = 0.16$. In the condition with locational uncertainty, there were significant congruency effects both in the evaluative decision task, $t(15) = 3.80$, $p < .01$, and the gender decision task, $t(15) = 2.99$, $p < .01$. Under locational certainty, there were no significant congruency effects (all $t < 1$). None of the balancing variables (order in which participants had to deal with the two tasks, response key assignment in the evaluative decision task, and response key assignment in the gender decision task) had any significant effect on the size of the congruency effects when entered into the analysis of variance. There were also no interactions between any of the balancing and the other independent variables.

To analyse whether absolute error percentages were dependent on locational uncertainty, kind of material, and kind of pair, an analysis of variance with the within-subjects factors "task" (evaluative decision on adjectives versus gender decision on names), "kind of pair" (congruent, incongruent, neutral), and the between-subjects factor "locational uncertainty" was performed on the absolute error percentages (see Table 1). It showed a main effect of task; more errors were made in the evaluative decision task than in the gender decision task, $F(1, 30) = 5.39$, $p < .03$. The main effect of locational uncertainty was also significant; more errors were made when the location of the target was uncertain, $F(1, 30) = 15.21$, $p < .01$. There was also a significant main effect of kind of pair, $F(2, 60) = 8.81$, $p < .01$. Additionally, there was a two-way interaction between kind of pair and task, $F(2, 60) = 8.14$, $p < .01$, and a three-way interaction between locational uncertainty, kind of pair, and task, $F(2, 60) = 5.53$, $p < .01$. The two latter effects were caused by a slightly enhanced number of errors when neutral adjective pairs were judged under locational uncertainty.

To test whether there was facilitation by congruent distractors, planned contrasts were performed. There was no significant difference in the number of errors between congruent and neutral trials under locational certainty or uncertainty; this was true both for the evaluative decision task and the gender decision task (all $ts < 1.2$). Thus, in no condition was the processing of congruent trials facilitated as compared to the baseline of neutral trials.

To test whether there was inhibition by incongruent distractors, error percentages were contrasted between incongruent and neutral pairs. Under locational uncertainty, there was a significant inhibition effect both in the evaluative decision task, $t(15) = 2.41$, $p < .02$ (one-tailed), and in the gender decision task, $t(15) = 4.74$, $p < .01$ (one-tailed). Under locational certainty, there was no significant inhibition effect. Thus, as can be seen in Table 1, inhibition effects were restricted to the distributed-attention condition.

Discussion

The results are clear-cut. Locational uncertainty had a significant effect on the magnitude of the effective congruency effect which was not moderated by the kind of material used (valenced vs. versus gender names). Substantial congruency effects of affect and gender occurred in the distributed-attention condition which left participants uncertain of the precise target location. No congruency effects were observed in the focused-attention condition. The closely parallel effects in the gender decision task suggest that the underlying mechanism is a rather general one that is not restricted to the evaluative stimulus dimension.

The automatic affective congruency effects in the distributed-attention condition are consistent with previous findings in the standard evaluative decision task (e.g., Bargh et al., 1992; Fazio et al., 1986; Hermans et al., 1994; Klauer et al., 1997). The presentation parameters in these previous experiments are comparable to the distributed-attention condition in the present study inasmuch as either procedure—presenting distractor and target on the same location or presenting distractor and target on unpredictable locations, but under distributed attention—ensures that some amount of attention must be directed toward the distractor stimulus. In contrast, there was no affective congruency effect in the focused-attention condition with locational certainty for the target. This effect of locational uncertainty closely mirrors similar effects in Stroop tasks (Kahneman et al., 1983; Paquet & Lortie, 1990; Underwood, 1976; Yantis & Johnston, 1990) and supports the proposed Stroop analogy of affective priming effects.

Of course, the results do not rule out that the affective priming effect is a kind of semantic priming effect. However, the results show that inhibition rather than facilitation caused the congruency effects under locational uncertainty. This preponderance of inhibition as compared to facilitation is a pattern that is also often observed in Stroop tasks (MacLeod, 1991). It supports the notion that the evaluative decision task at short SOAs can be conceptualised as a flanker task: The distractor stimuli have to be ignored to favour an action to the target; response competition and the subsequent selective inhibition of the distractor stimulus are the mechanisms that most likely have caused the observed congruency effects.

More errors were made under locational uncertainty than under locational certainty. Although this effect resembles the finding of increased naming latencies under locational uncertainty in the picture-word variant of the Stroop task (Underwood, 1976), it gives rise to a possible objection against the interpretation of the results sketched earlier. One may suspect that the moderating role of locational uncertainty is a scale artefact because participants in the focused-attention condition operated in a more sensitive region of the percentage correct scale. However, the observed effect is opposite to the direction that would have been expected if this reasoning were correct: approaching the ceiling of the chance baseline of 50% errors in the distributed-attention condition should have reduced rather than enhanced affective congruency effects.

Another objection that can be raised against the interpretation of the results of Experiment 1 is more difficult to refute. The visual cue in the focused-attention condition was presented to optimise the participant's ability to shift attention to the location of the target while simultaneously allowing them to narrow down the size of their attentional focus. As Remington (1980) has shown, visual cues can, however, trigger both an automatic shift of attention and an eye movement towards the cue. This link between attentional shifts and eye movements suggests an alternative explanation of the observed results based on retinal rather than attentional factors: Participants may have moved their eyes to the target location after the cue appeared. If so, the target word was presented foveally whereas the prime word was not, and differences in retinal acuity rather than differences in the distribution of attention may have caused the observed effect (Hagenaar & van der Heijden, 1986).

Although overt changes attention in everyday life are often accompanied by head and eye movements, the possibility of covert orientation of attention without moving the eyes is firmly established. William James cites an early experiment by Helmholtz who concluded that "our attention is quite independent of the position and accommodation of the eyes" (James, 1890, p. 438). There is now ample evidence that attention can be moved around the visual field without change in the point of fixation (see Johnston & Dark, 1986, for a review). Despite a large body of research demonstrating the possibility of covert shifts of attention without overt eye movements (Jonides, 1983; Posner, 1980; Rizzolatti, Riggio, Dascola, & Umilta, 1987; Shepherd, Findlay, & Hockey,

1986), changes of fixation toward the target in Experiment 1 cannot be ruled out. Experiment 2 investigated whether the effect of locational uncertainty was due to attention or eye movements.

EXPERIMENT 2

The normal latency of saccadic jumps induced by a stimulus outside of the fovea is about 220 ms (Bargh, 2000). Thus, when the precue precedes the target stimulus by 600 ms as in Experiment 1, the participant can change his/her fixation from the point corresponding to the centre of the display to the designated position of the target stimulus. Such a change in fixation would result in the target falling on a more sensitive foveal region with better identification performance (Inhoff & Rayner, 1980).

One possibility to directly examine this issue is to monitor eye movements by means of suitable apparatus and to restrict analysis to trials in which the eyes remain fixated. Another possibility is to reduce precue-target SOA to prevent participants from changing fixation. This is the approach taken in Experiment 2. It was conducted as an exact replication of Experiment 1 with the sole exception that precue SOA was reduced from 600 ms to 150 ms to control for eye movements. This procedural change eliminates participants' ability to move fixation to the designated target position because a 150 ms precue-target SOA is too short an interval for the participants to change fixation from the central fixation point to the position of the target (Bargh, 2000; Colegate, Hoffman, & Eriksen, 1973; Francolini & Egeth, 1980; Rayner, 1978). If different modes of attention rather than eye movements have caused the effect of locational uncertainty in Experiment 1, the effect should nevertheless be replicable with a short precue-target SOA of 150 ms.

Method

All stimuli and procedures were identical to Experiment 1. The only exception was that precue-target SOA was reduced from 600 ms to 150 ms to control for eye movements. To keep the speed of trial presentation constant despite the shorter SOA, the intertrial interval was increased by 450 ms.

Participants were 32 University of Bonn students from different faculties and nonstudent volunteers of a similar age range recruited by the experimenters. Psychology students received partial course credit. Students from other faculties were paid DM 10 (approx. US $6) for their participation, and nonstudent volunteers participated in exchange for detailed individual feedback on their results. All participants were native speakers of German and had normal or corrected-to-normal vision.

Results

Congruency effects in the evaluative decision task and the gender decision task were computed by subtracting percent correct for trials with incongruent pairs from percentage correct for trials with congruent pairs. Table 2 shows the congruency effects in both tasks as a function of locational uncertainty.

An analysis of variance with the within-subjects factor "task" (evaluative decision vs. gender decision) and the between-subjects factor "locational uncertainty" was performed on the congruency effects. There was a significant effect of locational uncertainty, $F(1, 30) = 11.63$, $p < .01$, but no effect of task (evaluative decision vs. gender decision), $F(1, 30) = 0.02$. The interaction of task and locational uncertainty was also not significant, $F(1, 30) = 1.04$. In the condition with locational uncertainty, there were significant congruency effects both in the evaluative decision task, $t(15) = 2.70$, $p < .02$, and the gender decision task, $t(15) = 3.58$, $p < .01$. Under locational certainty, there were no significant congruency effects (all $t < 1$). Thus, as in Experiment 1, there were significant congruency effects in both tasks, but they were restricted to the distributed-attention condition. None of the balancing variables (order in which participants had to deal with the two kinds of material, response key assignment in the evaluative decision task, and response key assignment in the gender decision task) had any significant effect on the size of the congruency effects when entered into the analysis of variance. Nor were there interactions between any of the balancing and the other independent variables.

An additional analysis of variance was performed on the pooled data of Experiments 1 and 2 to check whether possible changes of fixation enhance the effects of locational uncertainty. In this case, an interaction between locational uncertainty and precue SOA (600 ms in Experiment 1 vs. 150 ms in Experiment 2) should have been observed. However, no such interaction emerged ($F < 1$).

TABLE 2

Percentage errors and congruency effects (and standard deviations) in Experiment 2 as a function of the kind of material, locational uncertainty, and kind of pair

Material	Location	Kind of pair			Congruency effect
		Congruent	Neutral	Incongruent	
Adjectives	Uncertain	41.3 (8.4)	42.9 (9.6)	44.6 (9.2)	3.3 (4.9)
	Certain	38.0 (11.3)	38.8 (12.1)	38.9 (11.4)	0.9 (5.0)
Names	Uncertain	37.7 (11.3)	38.4 (10.9)	42.6 (11.7)	4.9 (5.4)
	Certain	31.4 (10.7)	31.8 (11.7)	31.3 (10.9)	−0.2 (3.8)

Note: Congruency effects were computed as the percentage errors difference between incongruent and congruent pairs.

In Table 2, absolute error percentages are shown as a function of locational uncertainty, kind of material (adjectives vs. names) and kind of pair (congruent, incongruent, and neutral). An analysis of variance with the within-subjects factors "task" (evaluative decision on adjectives vs. gender decision on names), "kind of pair" (congruent, incongruent, neutral), and the between-subjects factor "locational uncertainty" was performed on the absolute error percentages. It showed a main effect of task; more errors were made in the evaluative decision task than in the gender decision task, $F(1, 30) = 9.44$, $p < .01$. There was also a significant main effect of kind of pair, $F(1, 60) = 13.55$, $p < .01$. Contrary to Experiment 1, the main effect of locational uncertainty failed to reach significance, $F(1, 30) = 3.19$, $p > .08$. There was a significant two-way interaction between kind of trial and locational uncertainty, $F(1, 60) = 3.47$, $p < .04$.

To test for possible facilitation by congruent distractors, planned contrasts were performed. Neither under locational uncertainty, nor under locational certainty was there a significant difference in the number of errors between congruent and neutral trials; this was true both for the evaluative decision task and the gender decision task (all $ts < 1$). Thus, in no condition was the processing of congruent trials facilitated as compared to the baseline of neutral trials.

To test whether there was inhibition by incongruent distractors, error percentages were contrasted between incongruent and neutral trials. Under locational uncertainty, a significant inhibition effect occurred in the gender decision task, $t(15) = 2.03$, $p < .04$ (one-tailed). There was also evidence for inhibition in the evaluative decision task, but it did not reach the conventional level of significance, $t(15) = 1.06$, $p = .15$ (one-tailed). As in Experiment 1, no inhibition effects occurred under locational certainty (both $ts < 1$; see Table 2).

Discussion

In Experiment 1, precue-target SOA was 600 ms, which is sufficient to allow eye movements. If participants had moved their eyes to fixate the target words, the distractors would have fallen further from the fovea than the targets and the worse visibility of the distractors could have artefactually produced an apparent effect of locational uncertainty. Experiment 2 ruled out this alternative explanation, however. The results show that presenting a precue 150 ms before the target is sufficient to permit effective focusing of attention although this SOA is too short to allow initiation of eye movements. Thus, the effects of locational uncertainty appear to reflect covert allocation of attention rather than overt movements of the eyes. It seems safe to conclude that different sizes of attentional focus underlie the observed effects of locational uncertainty.

This reasoning is confirmed by the results of the analysis of variance on the pooled data from both experiments. If changes in fixation are necessary for effects of locational uncertainty to occur, this should be revealed by an interaction between locational uncertainty and precue SOA. However, there was no such interaction. This finding contradicts the notion that a fixation change was responsible for, or contributed to, the effect of locational uncertainty.

The finding of Experiment 1 that a significantly higher number of errors occurs under locational uncertainty than under locational certainty did not replicate in Experiment 2. Nevertheless, there was again a moderating effect of locational uncertainty on the size of affective congruency effects. This finding provides further evidence against the alternative interpretation already refuted earlier that the effect of locational uncertainty is a scale artefact due to overall differences between uncertainty conditions on the percentage correct scale.

GENERAL DISCUSSION

Affective congruency effects in the evaluative decision task have often been interpreted as evidence for the operation of an automatic evaluation process that is triggered by any valenced attitude object and that can influence the processing of any subsequently encountered stimuli. The results of the present experiments suggest that the effects of the automatic evaluation of incoming stimuli may be less far-reaching than has sometimes been assumed. In particular, our results show that affective congruency effects are not unavoidable and uncontrollable, but require attentional resources in addition to the triggering stimuli. Thus, despite the undisputed evidence that affective congruency effects are automatic by some criteria (e.g., Bargh, 1994; Draine & Greenwald, 1998), they nevertheless are susceptible to interference and influences of attention. Under appropriate conditions, automatic affective congruency effects can depend on the strategic spatial deployment of allocational resources.

A number of authors have assumed that there might be different modules for the processing of affective and nonaffective material or similarly that both kinds of processing might follow different laws (e.g., Bargh, 1997; Zajonc, 1980). In the present experiments, a control task was realised in which the evaluatively polarised words were replaced by first names, and the evaluative decision task was replaced by a gender decision task. There was no evidence for a special role or separate laws for the processing of evaluative material versus gender.

As predicted, in both of the present experiments the size of the effect of prime or distractor stimuli was moderated by attention. The results confirm that considerable processing of parafoveal prime words takes place when participants are not informed in advance of the precise target location. Obviously, under positional uncertainty, participants experience difficulty in restricting their attention to the target location, and affective congruency effects emerge. However, participants in the focused-attention group of either experiment showed impressive evidence of being able to prevent peripheral stimuli from interfering with performance. This result suggests that the evaluative decision task and flanker or Stroop tasks have much more in common than has originally been assumed (Fazio et al., 1986). The converging effects of locational uncertainty in the two paradigms add to the growing evidence that the parallels drawn between those tasks are well-founded (Klauer, 1998; Klauer et al., 1997; Klauer & Musch, 1999; Klinger et al., in press; Rothermund & Wentura, 1998; Wentura, 1999). The evaluative decision task and Stroop-like flanker tasks can be seen as special cases of a general model which assumes a weighted decision on the basis of evidence from different sources to which attention can either be allocated or be withhold from.

In situations in which narrowing the attentional focus to the target is possible and useful to fulfil current task demands, affective congruency effects may not occur as suggested by the present results. Although the present results do not rule out the possibility that the valence of unattended primes has been processed, they show that under appropriate conditions the response to the target is unaffected by the valence of the primes. The results also suggest that if task demands do not permit or encourage complete focusing of attention, affective congruency effects may be unavoidable. Whether affective congruency effects occur thus seems to depend on how difficult and how useful it is to narrow the focus of attention in a given situation.

Costs and benefits of distributed versus focused attention may vary with task demands and environment context even if no precue is given. If a target word is presented at a fixed location and distractor words are presented at random locations nearby, a high proportion of evaluatively congruent word pairs should encourage distributed attention to make use of the useful information the distractor provides about the valence of the target (Logan & Zbrodoff, 1979). Strong affective congruency effects can be expected in this condition. On the other hand, in a condition with identical presentation parameters, but with a low proportion of evaluatively congruent pairs, focusing attention on the target should enable participants to resist the influence of the irrelevant distractor. Klauer et al. (1997) have shown that in the standard evaluative decision task, affective congruency effects increase with increasing proportion of evaluatively congruent pairs. However, affective congruency effects were still significant when only 25% of trials were evaluatively incongruent and ignoring the distracting prime completely (or even giving it a negative weight) would have been an optimal strategy. Klauer et al. (1997) interpreted this finding as evidence for the automatic evaluation of the distractor is not under participants' control and cannot be suppressed. Based on the present findings, it can be predicted that when two words are presented at different locations, focusing attention on the target may completely eliminate affective congruency effects when consistency proportion is low.

Because the existence of affective congruency effects in the evaluative decision task is one of the cornerstones of automatic activation models (Bargh et al., 1992; Fazio et al., 1986), the observed effects of locational uncertainty are remarkable for theoretical reasons. Although it has traditionally been assumed that the automatic processes underlying Stroop and priming effects may be beyond control, there is growing evidence that they can in fact be closely controlled under appropriate conditions (Klauer et al., 1997; Logan, 1980). A converging conclusion was reached in the research on reflexes, which in many ways are the paradigm case of automaticity. Studies on the blink reflex have shown that reflexes can be modified by attention (Anthony, 1985). This and other findings show that so-called automatic processing does not seem to be as impervious to cognitive control as has often been assumed. If innate reflexes, such as the blink reflex, can be modified by attention, there is little reason to expect that Stroop effects and affective congruency effects do not also depend on attentional factors. One should also bear in mind that the orienting of attention in the context of an organism's familiar, natural environment contrasts sharply with the decontextualised situation in a typical laboratory experiment with sequential presentation of stimuli to the same place of the retina. Controlled automaticity may well be the rule rather than the exception in settings which are more ecologically valid than the traditional laboratory experiment.

Manuscript received 29 April 1999
Revised manuscript received 29 November 1999

REFERENCES

Anthony, B.J. (1985). In the blink of an eye: Implication of reflex modification for information processing. In P.K. Ackles, J.R. Jennings, & M.G.H. Coles (Eds.), *Advances in psychophysiology*, (Vol. 1, pp. 167–218). Greenwhich, CT: JAI Press.

Bargh, J.A. (1989). Conditional automaticity: Varieties of automatic influence in social perception and cognition. In J.S. Uleman & J.A. Bargh (Eds.), *Unintended thought* (pp. 3–51). New York: Guilford Press.

Bargh, J.A. (1994). The four horsemen of automaticity: Awareness, intention, efficiency, and control in social cognition. In R.S. Wyer & T.K. Srull (Eds.), *Handbook of social cognition* (Vol. 1, pp. 1–40). Hillsdale, NJ: Erlbaum.

Bargh, J.A. (1997). The automaticity of everyday life. In R.S. Wyer (Ed.), *Advances in social cognition* (Vol. 10, pp. 1–49). Mahwah, NJ: Erlbaum.

Bargh, J.A. (2000). A practical guide to priming and automaticity research. In H. Reis & C. Judd (Eds.), *Handbook of research methods in social psychology*. New York: Cambridge University Press.

Bargh, J.A., Chaiken, S., Govender, R., & Pratto, F. (1992). The generality of the automatic attitude activation effect. *Journal of Personality and Social Psychology, 62*, 893–912.

Bargh, J.A., Chaiken, S., Raymond, P., & Hymes, C. (1996). The automatic evaluation effect: Unconditional automatic attitude activation with a pronunciation task. *Journal of Experimental Social Psychology, 32*, 104–128.

Besner, D., Stolz, J., & Boutilier, C. (1997). The Stroop effect and the myth of automaticity. *Psychonomic Bulletin and Review, 4*, 221–225.

Besner, D., & Stolz, J. (1999). What kind of attention modulates the Stroop effect? *Psychonomic Bulletin and Review, 6*, 99–104.

Blair, I., & Banaji, M. (1996). Automatic and controlled processes in stereotype priming. *Journal of Personality and Social Psychology, 70*, 1142–1163.

Butler, B. (1974). The limits of selective attention in tachistoscopic recognition. *Canadian Journal of Psychology, 28* , 199–213.

Chaiken, S., & Bargh, J.A. (1993). Occurrence versus moderation of the automatic attitude activation effect: Reply to Fazio. *Journal of Personality and Social Psychology, 64*, 759–765.

Chen, M., & Bargh, J.A. (1999). Consequences of automatic evaluation: Immediate behavioral predispositions to approach or avoid the stimulus. *Personality and Social Psychology Bulletin, 25*, 215–224.

Colegate, R., Hoffman, J.E., & Eriksen, C.W. (1973). Selective encoding from multielement visual displays. *Perception and Psychophysics, 14*, 217–224.

De Houwer, J., & Hermans, D. (1999, June). *Nine attempts to find affective priming of pronunciation responses: Effects of SOA, degradation, and language*. Paper presented to the 7th Tagung der Fachgruppe Sozialpsychologie in Kassel, Germany.

De Houwer, J., Hermans, D., & Eelen, P. (1998a). Affective and identity priming with episodically associated stimuli. *Cognition and Emotion, 12*, 145–169.

De Houwer, J., Hermans, D., Rothermund, K., & Wentura, D. (1998b). *Affective priming of semantic categorization responses: A test of subordinate accounts of affective priming*. Manuscript submitted for publication.

Draine, S.C., & Greenwald, A.G. (1998). Replicable unconscious semantic priming. *Journal of Experimental Psychology: General, 127*, 286–303.

Duncan, J. (1980). The locus of interference in the perception of simultaneous stimuli. *Psychological Review, 87*, 272–300.

Eriksen, B.A., & Eriksen, C.W. (1974). Effects of noise letters upon the identification of a target letter in a nonsearch task. *Perception and Psychophysics, 16*, 143–149.

Eriksen, C.W., & Shultz, D.W. (1979). Information processing in visual search: A continuous flow conception and experimental results. *Perception and Psychophysics, 25*, 249–263.

Eriksen, C.W., & Yeh, Y.Y. (1985). Allocation of attention in the visual field. *Journal of Experimental Psychology: Human Perception and Performance, 5*, 583–598.

Fazio, R.H. (1993). Variability in the likelihood of automatic attitude activation: Data reanalysis and commentary on Bargh, Chaiken, Govender, & Pratto (1992). *Journal of Personality and Social Psychology, 18*, 753–758.

Fazio, R.H., Sanbonmatsu, D.M., Powell, M.C., & Kardes, F.R. (1986). On the automatic activation of attitudes. *Journal of Personality and Social Psychology, 50*, 229–238.

Francolini, C.M., & Egeth, H. (1980). On the non-automaticity of "automatic" activation: Evidence of selective seeing. *Perception and Psychophysics, 27*, 331–342.

Franks, J.J., Roskos-Ewoldsen, D.R., Bilbrey, C.W., & Roskos-Ewoldsen, B. (1998). *Artifacts in attitude priming research*. Unpublished manuscript.

Gatti, S.V ., & Egeth, H. (1978). Failure of spatial selectivity in vision. *Bulletin of the Psychonomic Society, 11*, 181–184.

Glaser, J., & Banaji, M.R. (1999). When fair is foul and foul is fair: Reverse priming in automatic evaluation. *Journal of Personality and Social Psychology, 77*, 669–687.

Greenwald, A.G., Draine, S.C., & Abrams, R.L. (1996). Three cognitive markers of unconscious semantic activation. *Science, 273*, 1699–1702.

Greenwald, A.G., Klinger, M.R., & Liu, T.J. (1989). Unconscious processing of dichoptically masked words. *Memory and Cognition, 17*, 35–47.

Hagenaar, R., & van der Heijden, A.H.C. (1986). Target-noise separation in visual selective attention. *Acta Psychologica, 62*, 161–176.

Haussmann, R.E. (1992). Tachistoscopic presentation and millisecond timing on the IBM PC/XT/AT and PS/2: A Turbo Pascal unit to provide general-purpose routines for CGA, Hercules, EGA, and VGA monitors. *Behavior Research Methods, Instruments, and Computers, 24*, 303–310.

Hermans, D. (1996). *Automatische stimulusevaluatie. Een experimentele analyse van de voorwaarden voor evaluatieve stimulusdiscriminatie aan de hand van het affectieve-primingparadigma* [Automatic stimulus evaluation. An experimental analysis of the preconditions for evaluative stimulus discrimination using an affective priming paradigm]. Unpublished PhD thesis, University of Leuven, Belgium.

Hermans, D., De Houwer, J., & Eelen, P. (1994). The affective priming effect: Automatic activation of evaluative information in memory. *Cognition and Emotion, 8,* 515–533.

Hermans, D., De Houwer, J., & Eelen, P. (1996). Evaluative decision latencies mediated by induced affective states. *Behaviour Research and Therapy, 34,* 483–488.

Hermans, D., Van den Broeck, A., & Eelen, P. (1998). Affective priming using a colour-naming task: A test of an affective-motivational account of affective priming effects. *Zeitschrift für Experimentelle Psychologie, 45,* 136–148.

Hill, A.B., & Kemp-Wheeler, S.M. (1989). The influence of context on lexical decision time for emotional and non-emotional words. *Current Psychology: Research and Reviews, 8,* 219–227.

Inhoff, A.W., & Rayner, K. (1980). Parafoveal word perception: A case against semantic pre-processing. *Perception and Psychophysics, 27,* 457–464.

James, W. (1950). *The principles of psychology.* New York: Dover. (Original work published 1890).

Johnston, W.A., & Dark, V.J. (1986). Selective attention. *Annual Review of Psychology, 37,* 43–75.

Jonides, J. (1983). Further toward a model of the mind's eye's movements. *Bulletin of the Psychonomic Society, 21,* 247–250.

Kahneman, D., & Henik, A. (1981). Perceptual organization and attention. In M. Kubovy & J.R. Pomerantz (Eds.), *Perceptual organization* (pp. 181–211). Hillsdale, NJ: Erlbaum.

Kahneman, D.A., & Treisman, A. (1984). Changing views of attention and automaticity. In R. Parasuraman & D.R. Davies (Eds.), *Varieties of attention* (pp. 29–61). New York: Academic Press.

Kahneman, D., Treisman, A., & Burkell, J. (1983). The cost of visual filtering. *Journal of Experimental Psychology: Human Perception and Performance, 9,* 510–522.

Klauer, K.C. (1998). Affective priming. *European Review of Social Psychology, 8,* 63–107.

Klauer, K.C., & Musch, J. (1998). *Evidence for no affective priming in the naming task.* Poster presented to the 10th Annual Convention of the American Psychological Society in Washington, DC, May 21–24. [WWW document]. Available URL: http://www.psychologie.uni-bonn.de/sozial/forsch/naming.htm.

Klauer, K.C., & Musch, J. (1999). *Goal-dependent and goal-independent effects of irrelevant evaluations.* Manuscript submitted for publication.

Klauer, K.C., Rossnagel, C., & Musch, J. (1997). List-context effects in evaluative priming. *Journal of Experimental Psychology: Learning, Memory and Cognition, 23,* 246–255.

Klinger, M., Burton, P., & Pitts, G. (in press). Mechanisms of unconscious priming: I. Response competition not spreading activation. *Journal of Experimental Psychology: Learning, Memory, and Cognition.*

LaBerge, D. (1983). Spatial extent of attention to letters and words. *Journal of Experimental Psychology: Human Perception and Performance, 9,* 371–379.

LaBerge, D., Carlson, R.L., Williams, J.K., & Bunney, B.G. (1997). Shifting attention in visual space: Tests of moving-spotlight models versus an activity-distribution model. *Journal of Experimental Psychology: Human Perception and Performance, 23,* 1380–1392.

Logan, G.D. (1980). Attention and automaticity in Stroop and priming tasks: Theory and data. *Cognitive Psychology, 12,* 523–553.

Logan, G.D., & Zbrodoff, N.J. (1979). When it helps to be misled: Facilitative effects of increasing the frequency of conflicting stimuli in a Stroop-like task. *Memory and Cognition, 7,* 166–174.

Logan, G.D., & Zbrodoff, N.J. (1982). Constraints on strategy construction in a speeded discrimination task. *Journal of Experimental Psychology: Human Perception and Performance, 8,* 502–520.

MacLeod, C.M. (1991). Half a century of research on the Stroop effect: An integrative review. *Psychological Bulletin, 109,* 163–203.

Macrae, C.N., Bodenhausen, G.V., Milne, A.B., Thorn, T.M.J., & Castelli, L. (1997). On the activation of social stereotypes: The moderating role of processing objectives. *Journal of Experimental Social Psychology*, *72*, 791–809.

Müller, H.J., & Rabbitt, P.M.A. (1989). Reflexive and voluntary orienting of visual attention: Time course of activation and resistance to interruption. *Journal of Experimental Psychology: Human Perception and Performance*, *15*, 315–330.

Murphy, S.T., & Zajonc, R.B. (1993). Affect, cognition, and awareness: Affective priming with optimal and suboptimal stimulus exposure. *Journal of Personality and Social Psychology*, *64*, 723–739.

Musch, J., & Klauer, K.C. (1997). Der Anteilseffekt beim affektiven Priming: Replikation und Bewertung einer theoretischen Erklärung [The proportion effect in affective priming: Replication and evaluation of a theoretical framework]. *Zeitschrift für Experimentelle Psychologie*, *44*, 266–292.

Paquet, L., & Lortie, C. (1990). Evidence for early selection: Precuing target location reduced interference from same-category distractors. *Perception and Psychophysics*, *48*, 382–388.

Posner, M.I. (1980). Orienting of attention. *Quarterly Journal of Experimental Psychology*, *32*, 3–25.

Posner, M.I., & Boies, S.J. (1971). Components of attention. *Psychological Review*, *78*, 391–408.

Posner, M.I., Snyder, C.lR., & Davidson, B.J. (1980). Attention and the detection of signals. *Journal of Experimental Psychology: General*, *109*, 160–174.

Rayner, K. (1978). Eye movement latencies for parafoveally presented words. *Bulletin of the Psychonomic Society*, *11*, 13–16.

Remington, R.W. (1980). Attention and saccadic eye movements. *Journal of Experimental Psychology: Human Perception and Performance*, *6*, 726–744.

Rizzolatti, G., Riggio, L., Dascola, I., & Umilta, C. (1987). Reorienting attention across the horizontal and vertical meridians: evidence in favor of a premotor theory of attention. *Neuropsychologia*, *25*, 31–40.

Rothermund, K., & Wentura, D. (1998). Ein fairer Test für die Aktivationsausbreitungshypothese: affektives Priming in der Stroop-Aufgabe [An unbiased test of a spreading activation account of affective priming: Analysis of affective congruency effects in the Stroop task]. *Zeitschrit für Experimentelle Psycholmogie*, *45*, 120–135.

Shepherd, M., Findlay, J.M., & Hockey, R.J. (1986). The relationship between eye movements and spatial attention. *Quarterly Journal of Experimental Psychology*, *38A*, 475–491.

Taylor, S.E., Fiske, S.T., Etcoff, N.J., & Ruderman, A.J. (1978). Categorical and contextual bases of person memory and stereotyping. *Journal of Personality and Social Psychology*, *36*, 778–793.

Umilta, C. (1988). Orienting of attention. In F. Boller & J. Grafman (Eds.), *Handbook of neuropsychology* (Vol. 1, pp. 175–193). Amsterdam: Elsevier.

Underwood, G. (1976). Semantic interference from unattended printed words. *British Journal of Psychology*, *67*, 327–338.

Voorgang, D. (1994). *Die schönsten Vornamen* [The most beautiful first names]. Niedernhausen: Falken.

Wentura, D. (1998). Affektives Priming in der Wortentscheidungsaufgabe: Evidenz für postlexikalische Urteilstendenzen [Affective priming in the lexical decision task: Evidence for postlexical judgemental tendencies]. *Sprache und Kognition*, *17*, 125–137.

Wentura, D. (1999). Activation and inhibition of affective information: Evidence for negative priming in the evaluation task. *Cognition and Emotion*, *13*, 65–91.

Yantis, S., & Johnston, J.C. (1990). On the locus of visual selection: Evidence from focused attention tasks. *Journal of Experimental Psychology: Human Perception and Performance*, *16*, 135–149.

Zajonc, R.B. (1980). Feeling and thinking: Preferences need no inferences. *American Psychologist*, *39*, 117–124.

COGNITION AND EMOTION, 2001, 15 (2), 189–206

On the generality of the affective Simon effect

Jan De Houwer

University of Southampton, UK

Geert Crombez

University of Ghent, Belgium

Frank Baeyens and Dirk Hermans

University of Leuven, Belgium

In affective Simon studies, participants are to select between a positive and negative response on the basis of a nonaffective stimulus feature (i.e., relevant stimulus feature) while ignoring the valence of the presented stimuli (i.e., irrelevant stimulus feature). De Houwer and Eelen (1998) showed that the time to select the correct response is influenced by the match between the valence of the response and the (irrelevant) valence of the stimulus. In the affective Simon studies that have been reported until now, only words were used as stimuli and the relevant stimulus feature was always the grammatical category of the words. We report four experiments in which we examined the generality of the affective Simon effect. Significant affective Simon effects were found when the semantic category, grammatical category, and letter-case of words was relevant, when the semantic category of photographed objects was relevant, and when participants were asked to give nonverbal approach or avoidance responses on the basis of the grammatical category of words. Results also showed that the magnitude of the affective Simon effect depended on the nature of the relevant feature.

Correspondence should be addressed to Jan De Houwer, Department of Psychology, University of Southampton, Highfield, Southampton SO17 1BJ, UK; e-mail JanDH@soton.ac.uk

Experiments 1–3 were conducted while Jan De Houwer was a research assistant for the Fund for Scientific (Flanders-Belgium) at the University of Leuven and Geert Crombez was a post-doctoral researcher for the Fund for Scientific (Flanders-Belgium) at the University of Leuven. Frank Baeyens and Dirk Hermans are post-doctoral researchers for the Fund for Scientific Research (Flanders, Belgium). Experiments 1–3 were part of Jan De Houwer's doctoral dissertation that was presented at the University of Leuven.

We would like to thank Roeland Smout and Bea Martin for their help in running the experiments and gratefully acknowledge the comments and input of Paul Eelen, John Bargh, Omer Van den Bergh, Géry d'Ydewalle, Bernhard Hommel, Klaus Rothermund, and an anonymous reviewer.

http://www.tandf.co.uk/journals/pp/02699931.html   DOI:10.1080/0269993004200051

De Houwer and Eelen (1998) recently reported a number of experiments in which they presented positive and negative nouns (e.g., baby, murder) and adjectives (e.g., happy, cruel) and asked participants to respond as fast as possible by saying a predetermined positive or negative word (e.g., POSITIVE or NEGATIVE) on the basis of the grammatical category of the presented word (i.e., noun or adjective). Half of the participants had to say POSITIVE to nouns and NEGATIVE to adjectives whereas the other half had to say NEGATIVE to nouns and POSITIVE to adjectives, regardless of the valence of the nouns and adjectives. Despite the fact that stimulus-valence was irrelevant and had to be ignored, reaction times were shorter when the valence of the presented word and the valence of the correct response matched compared to when valence differed. On the basis of this result, one can concluded that stimulus-valence was processed automatically in the sense of involuntary and efficiently (Bargh, 1992).[1]

At an abstract level, the paradigm that was used in the experiments reported by De Houwer and Eelen (1998) is highly similar to the spatial Simon paradigm (e.g., Lu & Proctor, 1995; Simon, 1990; Simon & Rudell, 1967). In spatial Simon studies, participants are asked to give a spatial response based on the identity of a nonspatial stimulus feature while ignoring the spatial location of the presented stimulus. Even though the spatial location of the relevant stimulus is irrelevant, results typically show that responses are faster when the spatial position of the stimulus corresponds to the spatial features of the response that has to be made. For instance, participants might be asked to press the left key of a button press device upon presentation of a red light and the right key upon presentation of a green light, irrespective of whether the light is presented on the left or right side of a visual display. In this case, responses to the red light will be faster when it is presented on the left side of the display than when it is presented on the right side. Responses to the green light will be faster when presented on the right side (e.g., Craft & Simon, 1970).

Both in the studies conducted by De Houwer and Eelen (1998) and in spatial Simon studies, three elements are of crucial importance: (1) a relevant feature that determines what the correct response should be (e.g., grammatical category or colour); (2) an irrelevant feature that has to be ignored (i.e., stimulus-valence or spatial location); and (3) responses (e.g., the words POSITIVE and NEGA-TIVE or a left or right key press) that are meaningfully related to the irrelevant feature but not to the relevant feature. Therefore, the paradigm that was used by De Houwer and Eelen can be regarded as an affective variant of the Simon

---

[1] Rather than adopting an "all or none" view on automaticity (e.g., Posner & Snyder, 1975; Shiffrin & Schneider, 1977), we take a conditional approach to automaticity which postulates that different types of automatic processes may exist, each with different characteristics (Bargh, 1992). For instance, a process that is automatic in the sense of involuntary may still depend on the prior activation of certain cognitive representations or certain goals.

paradigm.[2] The affective Simon paradigm differs from the original spatial Simon paradigm with regard to the nature of the irrelevant feature and the nature of the relation between the irrelevant feature and the responses. In an affective Simon paradigm, stimulus-valence is the irrelevant feature and the irrelevant feature and the responses are meaningfully related because both have affective properties. In a spatial Simon paradigm, the irrelevant feature is the spatial location of a stimulus and the responses also have spatial properties.

De Houwer and Eelen (1998) argue that the affective Simon paradigm offers a flexible tool for the study of automatic affective processing. For instance, one can use stimuli of different modalities and complexity and for each kind of stimuli, different relevant features can be used. In their experiments, De Houwer and Eelen, however, only used words as stimuli and grammatical category as relevant feature. Moreover, participants were always asked to give verbal responses. The question thus remains as to whether reliable affective Simon effects can be observed when other kinds of stimuli, relevant features, or responses are used. The aim of the experiments reported in this paper was to investigate the generalisability of the affective Simon effect. First, apart from words, we also used pictures of valenced objects as stimuli. Second, for words and pictures, we used several relevant features and examined whether the magnitude of the affective Simon effect was influenced by the nature of the relevant feature. Finally, we looked at whether affective Simon effects can also be observed when participants are asked to give nonverbal responses that are linked to avoidance or approach.

In Experiment 1, words were presented that corresponded to names of animals or persons with a positive (e.g., BUTTERFLY and FRIEND) or negative valence (e.g., COCKROACH and ENEMY). Participants had to use the semantic category to which a word belonged as a cue to respond with the word POSITIVE or NEGATIVE. Written words were also presented in Experiment 2, but now we manipulated the nature of the relevant feature. The first condition of Experiment 2 was an exact replication of a study previously reported by De Houwer and Eelen (1998, Experiment 2). Nouns and adjectives were presented and participants had to use the grammatical category of the words as a cue to respond. In the second condition, half of the nouns and adjectives were presented in lower-case letters and half in upper-case letters and letter-case was the relevant feature. In Experiment 3, black and white and color pictures of positive or negative man-made objects (e.g., a car, a toilet, a cake) or natural objects

---

[2] One might argue that the affective Simon task is more similar to a Stroop colour-word task than to a spatial Simon task because both the affective Simon and Stroop colour-word task involve irrelevant semantic information rather than spatial information. However, as was noted by Kornblum and Lee (1995) and De Houwer (in preparation), Stroop tasks are structurally different from both the affective and spatial Simon task because in Stroop but not Simon tasks, the relevant feature is meaningfully related to the responses and the irrelevant feature.

(e.g., a spider, clouds, a river) were presented. Half of the participants were instructed to say POSITIVE or NEGATIVE depending upon whether a picture of a man-made or natural object was presented. Other participants had to use the colour of the presented pictures (black and white or coloured) as a cue to respond. Finally, in Experiment 4, positive and negative nouns and adjectives were presented and participants were asked to move a manikin towards or away from the word depending on its grammatical category.

EXPERIMENT 1

This experiment was devised as a first test of the generalisability of the affective Simon effect. Whereas De Houwer and Eelen (1998) asked participants to say POSITIVE or NEGATIVE on the basis of the grammatical category of the presented nouns and adjectives, we asked participants to respond on the basis of the semantic category of words corresponding to animals or persons.

Method

Participants.   Sixteen first year psychology students (15 women, 1 man) at the University of Leuven participated for partial fulfilment of course requirements. As in all following experiments, all participants were native Dutch speakers.

Materials.   Twenty names of persons and twenty names of animals were used as experimental stimuli. Half of the person and animal names were assumed to have a positive valence, half were assumed to have a negative valence. Twenty additional words (10 person names and 10 animal names) were presented only during practice trials. All words were written in white upper-case letters on a black background and were presented on a 70 Hz SVGA screen connected to an IBM-compatible 486 computer. A letter was 7 mm high and 5 mm wide. Presentations were controlled by a Turbo Pascal 5.0 program that operated in graphics mode. Participants were seated in front of the computer screen at a distance of approximately 40 cm. Verbal responses were registered by a voice key which generated a signal that stopped a highly accurate (beyond 1 ms) Turbo Pascal Timer (Bovens & Brysbaert, 1990).

Procedure.   All participants were tested individually. Instructions were presented on the computer screen. Participants were asked to determine the semantic category (person or animal) of each presented word. Half were instructed to say the Dutch word POSITIEF (POSITIVE) as fast as possible on presentation of the name of a person and the Dutch word NEGATIEF (NEGATIVE) on presentation of an animal name. The opposite stimulus-response assignment was used for the other participants. All participants were informed that response times would be measured using a voice key. In order for the voice key to correctly register the responses, they were asked to respond clearly and to avoid making other sounds.

After the participant read the instructions, the 20 practice stimuli were presented once. Following a brief break, the 40 experimental stimuli were presented once. The experimental stimuli were presented a second time after a brief break. Each practice and experimental trial consisted of the following sequence of events: a warning tone (1000 Hz, 200 ms), a fixation cross (500 ms), a blank screen (500 ms), and a word that remained on the screen until the voice key registered a response. If no response was registered, the word disappeared automatically after 3000 ms. All visual stimuli (fixation cross and word) were presented in the middle of the computer screen. After each trial, the experimenter entered a code into the computer which corresponded to the response that was given, except on trials where the voice key failed to correctly register the response in which case a different code was entered. The next trial was initiated 1500 ms after the experimenter entered a code. The order in which the stimuli were presented was determined randomly with the restriction that no more than four words of the same semantic category could be presented consecutively. A separate randomisation was used for each participant and each (practice, experimental, and rating) block.

In order to check whether the selected positive words were indeed perceived as being more positive than the selected negative words, participants were asked to rate the valence of the 40 words that were presented during the experimental trials on a 1 (negative) to 7 (positive) scale. The ratings were obtained after all experimental stimuli had been presented.

Results and discussion

For each participant, the number of errors and the mean reaction time on congruent (the valence of the correct response and the presented word matched) and incongruent (the valence of the correct response and the presented word were opposite) experimental trials were calculated for the two experimental blocks separately. As in all subsequent experiments, a preliminary analysis showed that the effects of congruence were not significantly influenced by block and therefore the data were pooled over blocks. Reaction times on trials where: (a) an incorrect response was given, (b) a voice key failure occurred, or (c) a word was presented that was given an idiosyncratic rating, that is, a positive word that was rated by the participant as negative (a rating of 3 or less) or a negative word that was rated as positive (a rating of 5 or more) were not taken into account. F-tests were used to assess the effect of congruence on mean reaction times and number of errors. As in all following experiments, the significance level was set at $p < .05$.

Voice key failures occurred on 4.26% of all trials and incorrect responses were given on 2.57% of the remaining trials. On 4.28% of all trials, a word was presented that was given an idiosyncratic rating. Positive words were given a mean rating of 5.78 (SD = 0.48) and negative words were given a mean rating of 2.23 (SD = 0.33), $F(1, 15) = 722.77$, $MS_e = 0.14$. Mean reaction times and number of errors are displayed in Table 1.

Analyses showed that reaction times were significantly shorter on congruent than on incongruent trials, $F(1, 15) = 15.00$, $MS_e = 486.88$, but the number of errors was not significantly different on congruent than on incongruent trials, $F(1, 15) = 1.00$.

Results clearly showed that the time to say POSITIVE or NEGATIVE on the basis of the semantic category of the presented words was influenced by the (irrelevant) valence of the words. This result extends the findings reported by De Houwer and Eelen (1998) in showing that significant affective Simon effects can not only be found when grammatical category is the relevant feature, but also when the semantic category of the presented words is relevant. In a number of experiments in which non-student native English speakers participated, S. Chu (personal communication, 24 July 1997) also observed robust affective Simon effects when the semantic category (person vs. object) of words was relevant, a finding which attests to the reliability of the present result.

EXPERIMENT 2

In order to determine the semantic category of a word, one has to process intentionally the semantic meaning of the words. Likewise, it is likely that when participants have to determine the grammatical category of a word, semantic processing is also necessary (but see Levelt, 1989; Roelofs, 1992). Therefore, one could conclude that at present affective Simon effects have only been observed when relevant features are used that force or encourage participants to process the semantic meaning of the words intentionally. In the present experiment, we examined whether an affective Simon effect can also be observed when a relevant feature is used that can be determined on the basis of perceptual processing, thus rendering it unlikely that participants intentionally process the presented stimuli at a semantic level. Half of the participants saw words that were printed in upper-case or lower-case letters and were asked to say POSITIVE or NEGATIVE on the basis of the letter-case of the presented word. One can assume that participants will not have the intention of processing the semantic meaning of a word when they have to determine its letter-case, simply because knowledge of the semantic features of a word does not provide information about the letter-case of that word.

Although intentional semantic processing might not be necessary to obtain affective Simon effects, it is possible that the magnitude of the affective Simon effect does depend on whether or not the presented stimulus is intentionally processed at a semantic level. That is, it might be harder to ignore the valence of a stimulus when one intentionally processes the stimulus semantically compared to when the stimulus only has to be processed on a perceptual level. In order to examine this issue, we also ran a condition in which grammatical category was the relevant feature (grammatical condition) and compared the magnitude of the affective Simon effect in this condition with the magnitude of the effect in the condition where letter-case was relevant (letter-case condition).

Method

Participants.   Thirty-two second year psychology students (24 woman, 8 men) at the University of Leuven participated for partial fulfilment of course requirements.

Materials, procedure, and analyses.   On the basis of the normative study of Hermans and De Houwer (1994), we selected 10 positive (mean rating in the normative study = 6.00; SD = 0.40) and 10 negative (M = 1.73; SD = 0.27) nouns and 10 positive (M = 5.93; SD = 0.26) and 10 negative (M = 1.83; SD = 0.28) adjectives as experimental stimuli. In addition, five positive and five negative nouns and adjectives were selected as practice stimuli. These stimuli were the same as those used in a study previously reported by De Houwer and Eelen (1998, experiment 2).

In the grammatical condition, all words were presented in upper-case letters. Half of the participants who were assigned to the grammatical condition were asked to say the word POSITIVE as fast as possible when a noun was presented and to respond with the word NEGATIVE when an adjective was presented. The other participants were to say NEGATIVE on presentation of a noun and POSITIVE on presentation of an adjective. In the letter-case condition, the same words were presented as in the grammatical condition. However, half of the nouns and adjectives were written in lower-case letters, half were written in upper-case letters. Half of the words that were written in upper-case letters had a positive valence, half had a negative valence. The same was true for the words presented in lower-case letters. Half of the participants who were assigned to the letter-case condition were instructed to respond with the word POSITIVE on presentation of a word in lower-case letters and with the word NEGATIVE when the presented word consisted of upper-case letters. The response assignment was reversed for the other participants. Because selection of all stimuli was based on norms (Hermans & De Houwer, 1994), participants were not asked to rate the valence of the words at the end of the experiment. All other aspects of the materials and procedure were the same as in Experiment 1.

Results and discussion

Reaction times and errors were determined as in Experiment 1 except that idiosyncratic valence ratings could of course not be used as a criterion to exclude trials. Data were analysed using Condition (grammatical vs. letter-case) × Congruence (congruent vs. incongruent) ANOVAs. A priori F-tests were conducted to assess the effect of congruence in the grammatical and letter-case conditions separately.

Voice key failures occurred on 3.48% of all trials and incorrect responses were given on 3.40% of the remaining trials. Mean reaction times and number of errors are presented in Table 1. The analysis of reaction time data revealed a main effect of congruence, $F(1, 30) = 14.28$, $MS_e = 1323.93$, that interacted with condition, $F(1, 30) = 4.41$, $MS_e = 1313.93$. Table 1 shows that the effect of congruence was stronger in the grammatical condition than in the letter-case condition. A priori tests revealed that reaction times were significantly shorter on congruent than on incongruent trials in both the grammatical, $F(1, 15) = 10.10$, $MS_e = 2265.21$, and the letter-case condition, $F(1, 15) = 4.87$, $MS_e = 382.64$. The main effect of condition was also significant, $F(1, 30) = 73.55$, $MS_e = 13125.20$, showing longer reaction times in the grammatical condition than in the letter-case condition.

TABLE 1

Mean reaction times (in ms) and mean number of errors (SD in parentheses) as a function of congruence in Experiments 1, 2, 3, and 4

	Congruence	
Experiment	*Congruent*	*Incongruent*
Experiment 1		
Reaction time	632 (103)	663 (104)
Errors	0.56 (0.81)	0.94 (1.06)
Experiment 2		
Grammatical condition		
Reaction time	735 (102)	789 (106)
Errors	1.56 (2.16)	2.56 (1.46)
Letter-case condition		
Reaction time	509 (58)	524 (61)
Errors	0.56 (0.63)	0.56 (0.81)
Experiment 3		
Semantic condition		
Reaction time	820 (124)	855 (119)
Errors	0.89 (0.99)	0.63 (0.95)
Perceptual Condition		
Reaction time	665 (119)	667 (126)
Errors	0.28 (0.67)	0.56 (0.86)
Experiment 4		
Reaction time	987 (330)	1020 (339)
Errors	2.46 (3.13)	3.17 (2.92)

The analysis of error data did not reveal a significant main effect of congruence, $F(1, 30) = 1.76$, $MS_e = 2.27$, nor an interaction between congruence and condition, $F(1, 30) = 1.76$, $MS_e = 2.27$. The main effect of condition was significant, $F(1, 30) = 21.71$, $MS_e = 1.66$, showing that less errors were made in the letter-case condition than in the grammatical condition. A priori tests also did not reveal a main effect of congruence, neither in the grammatical condition, $F(1, 15) = 1.97$, $MS_e = 2.03$, nor in the letter-case condition, $F < 1$.

The most important result of the present experiment was the significant affective Simon effect that occurred in the letter-case condition. When participants had to select the correct response (POSITIVE or NEGATIVE) on the basis of the letter-case of the presented word, reaction times were shorter when the valence of the presented word and the correct response matched compared to when this differed. The effect occurred despite the fact that it is unlikely that participants processed the semantic meaning of the presented words intentionally. Therefore, the present results support the conclusion that intentional semantic processing of the stimuli is not necessary in order to obtain affective Simon effects.

Although the affective Simon effect was significant in the letter-case condition, the interaction between condition and congruence suggests that the affective Simon effect was significantly smaller when letter-case was relevant compared to when grammatical category was relevant. However, this interaction might have been due to the fact that reaction times were overall significantly longer in the grammatical condition than in the letter-case condition. It is well known that an increase in reaction time can cause an artificial increase in difference measures. This artefact can be removed by log-transforming the mean reaction times for each participant (Chapman, Chapman, Curran, & Miller, 1994).[3] A Condition × Congruence ANOVA which was performed on the log-transformed mean reaction times showed that the interaction between both variables no longer reached conventional levels of significance, $F(1, 30) = 2.71$, $MS_e = 0.003$, $p = .11$. Therefore, when statistically controlling for the artefact caused by differences in overall reaction times, we can no longer conclude that the magnitude of the affective Simon effect depended on the nature of the relevant feature.

EXPERIMENT 3

Both in the experiments reported by De Houwer and Eelen (1998) and in Experiments 1 and 2 of the present paper, words were used as stimuli. As a further test of the generality of the affective Simon effect, in Experiment 3, we examined whether significant affective Simon effects can also be found when pictures of valenced objects are used as stimuli. As in Experiment 2, we again

---

[3] The authors would like to thank Klaus Rothermund for pointing out this solution.

ran two conditions, one in which a semantic feature of the pictures was relevant (i.e., whether the depicted object was man-made or not) and one condition in which a perceptual feature of the pictures was relevant (i.e., whether the picture was a colour or black and white picture).

Method

Participants. Thirty-nine female first year psychology students at the University of Leuven participated for partial fulfilment of course requirements.

Materials. Stimuli were selected from the photographs included in the International Affective Picture System (IAPS) (Centre for the Study of Emotion and Attention, 1995; Lang, Bradley, & Cuthbert, 1995). The IAPS provides mean evaluation ratings on a scale from 1 (negative) to 9 (positive) for 364 pictures based on a sample of male and female Introductory Psychology students. We selected 16 pictures with a positive valence and 16 pictures with a negative valence on the basis of the evaluative ratings given by female participants in the IAPS normative study (Lang et al., 1995). Half of the selected positive and negative pictures depicted man-made objects (e.g., chocolate, a toilet), the other pictures depicted natural objects that are not man-made (e.g., a snake, flowers). Half of the positive and negative man-made and natural objects were presented using colour slides, half were presented using black and white slides. There were four experimental stimuli of each of the eight possible kinds of pictures: (1) positive valence, man-made, black and white, (2) positive valence, man-made, coloured, (3) positive valence, natural, black and white, (4) positive valence, natural, coloured, (5) negative valence, man-made, black and white, (6) negative valence, man-made, coloured, (7) negative valence, natural, black and white, (8) negative valence, natural, coloured. A Valence (positive vs. negative) × Semantic category (man-made vs. natural) × Colour (black and white vs. colour) ANOVA showed that the selected positive pictures ($M = 7.33$, $SD = 0.89$) where given a higher evaluative rating in the normative study (Lang et al., 1995) than the selected negative pictures ($M = 2.91$, $SD = 0.59$), $F(1, 24) = 723.55$, $MS_e = 0.25$. Overall, pictures of man-made objects ($M = 4.79$, $SD = 2.42$) were less positive than pictures of natural objects ($M = 5.58$, $SD = 2.60$), $F(1, 24) = 19.56$, $MS_e = 0.25$. No other effects were significant (all $Fs < 1$). We also selected one additional picture of each kind of picture. These eight additional pictures served as practice stimuli. Finally, a slide of a white cross on a black background was used to present a fixation cross at the beginning of each trial.

Slides were projected on the back of a ground glass screen using Kodak Ektapro 5000 slide projectors. Participants were seated at the other side of the screen at a distance of approximately 3 m. The projected pictures were either 66 cm high and 42 cm wide or 42 cm high and 66 cm wide. The slide projector was connected to an IBM-compatible XT computer. A Turbo Pascal 5.0 program controlled the selection of the slides and the opening and closing of the internal shutter of the Kodak Ektapro 5000. Verbal responses were registered by a voice key that generated a signal that stopped a highly accurate Turbo Pascal Timer (Bovens & Brysbaert, 1990). The experiment took place in a dimly lit room.

Procedure.   Participants were told that black and white pictures and colour pictures of man-made and natural objects would be presented. Half of the participants who were assigned to the perceptual condition were instructed to say POSITIVE on presentation of a black and white picture of an object and NEGATIVE when a colour picture of an object would be presented. The response assignment was reversed for the other participants in the perceptual condition. Half of the participants in the semantic condition were instructed to respond with the word POSITIVE following the presentation of a man-made object and to say NEGATIVE when a natural object was presented. The reverse was true for the remaining participants. In contrast to previous experiments, instructions were written down on a sheet that was handed over to the participant at the beginning of the experiment.

After instructions, the eight practice stimuli were presented twice. If participants gave an incorrect response on a practice trial, the experimenter drew attention to the error and repeated the instructions briefly. Then the 32 experimental stimuli were presented once in each of two consecutive blocks that were separated by a brief break. Each practice and experimental trial consisted of the following sequence of events: a warning tone (1000 Hz, 200 ms), a white fixation cross (500 ms), a delay during which the screen remained black (250 ms), and a picture that was presented until the voice key registered a response. If no response was registered, the picture disappeared automatically after 3000 ms. After each trial, a code was entered into the computer. The code corresponds to the response that was given, except on trials where the voice key failed to correctly register the response, in which case a separate code was entered. The next trial was initiated 3000 ms after the experimenter entered a code. The order of presentation was randomised separately for each participant and for each (practice and experimental) block with the restriction that no more than three consecutive pictures could depict an object of the same category (i.e., man-made or natural) or in the same colour (coloured or black and white).

In order to verify whether participants could identify the presented experimental stimuli and correctly perceived their valence and category, they were asked three questions about each experimental stimulus at the end of the experiment. First, they were to name the object that was shown. Second, they were asked to rate the valence of the object on a 1 (very negative) to 7 (very positive) scale. Third, they had to indicate the degree to which an object was natural or man-made on a 1 (natural) to 7 (man-made) scale.

Results and discussion

For each participant, mean reaction times and number of errors on congruent and incongruent experimental trials were calculated. Trials on which a voice key failure occurred, were not taken into account. Reaction times on trials where an incorrect response was given, were discarded. Finally, trials on which an object was shown that was: (a) named incorrectly or could not be recognised at the end of the experiment, or (b) was given an idiosyncratic affective rating (a positive object that was given a rating of 3 or less or a negative object that was given a rating of 5 or more), were discarded. The resulting data were analysed using a Condition (semantic vs. perceptual) × Congruence (congruent vs. incongruent) ANOVA. A priori F-tests were conducted to assess the effect of congruence in the semantic and perceptual condition separately.

One participant who was assigned to the semantic condition consistently rated all natural objects (including the negative natural objects) as very positive (a rating of 7). Her data were discarded from the analysis. The data of a second participant assigned to the perceptual condition were discarded because she gave an idiosyncratic affective rating for 18 stimuli, which exceeded the mean number of idiosyncratically rated or named objects in the perceptual condition ($M = 5.37$, SD $= 3.90$) by more than three standard deviations. Of the remaining 37 participants, 19 were assigned to the semantic condition and 18 were assigned to the perceptual condition. Voice key failures occurred on 3.21% of all trials. Incorrect responses were given on 1.92% of all remaining trials. Despite the fact that the stimuli were selected from the IAPS (Centre for the Study of Emotion and Attention, 1995; Lang et al., 1995), in 57 cases a stimulus could not be named correctly and in 143 cases a stimulus was given an idiosyncratic affective rating. Trials on which these stimuli were presented (16.90% of all trials) were discarded.[4]

All relevant means can be found in Table 1. The Condition × Congruence ANOVA of the reaction time data showed that reaction times were shorter in the perceptual condition than in the semantic condition, $F(1, 35) = 19.07$, $MS_e = 28577.40$, and that participants needed less time to respond on congruent than on incongruent trials, $F(1, 35) = 5.31$, $MS_e = 1228.72$. The interaction between condition and congruence also reached significance, $F(1, 35) = 4.18$, $MS_e = 1228.72$. A priori F-tests showed that the main effect of congruence was significant in the semantic condition, $F(1, 18) = 6.62$, $MS_e = 1803.72$, but not in the perceptual condition, $F < 1$. In order to investigate whether the interaction between condition and congruence was due to the large difference in overall reaction time between the two conditions, we also analysed the log-transformed

---

[4] When these data were included, ANOVAs revealed the same significant (albeit somewhat weaker) effects. Only the significant interaction between condition and congruence that was observed in the overall analysis of the reaction time data was reduced to a marginally significant interaction ($p < .10$).

mean reactions times. This analysis also revealed a significant interaction, $F(1, 35) = 4.37$, $MS_e = .002$.

The analysis of the error data only revealed a marginally significant main effect of condition, $F(1, 35) = 3.43$, $MS_e = 0.16$; $p = .072$, showing that the number of errors tended to be higher in the semantic condition than in the perceptual condition. However, the interaction between condition and congruence, $F(1, 35) = 1.50$, $MS_e = 0.22$, was not significant. F-tests did not reveal a significant effect of congruence, neither in the semantic nor in the perceptual conditions, $Fs < 1$.

First, a significant affective Simon effect was observed when participants had to decide whether the object was man-made or natural in order to select the correct response. This provides the first demonstration of an affective Simon effect when pictures of objects were used as stimuli and shows that such pictures can evoke automatic affective reactions (also see Hermans, De Houwer, & Eelen, 1994). Second, an affective Simon effect was only observed when a semantic feature of the presented pictures was relevant but not when a perceptual feature had to be processed in order to determine the correct response. This difference does not appear to be the result of an artefact caused by the longer reaction times in the semantic than in the perceptual condition because the interaction between condition and congruence was still significant when log-transformed means were analysed (Chapman et al., 1994). We will discuss this finding further in the general discussion.

EXPERIMENT 4

In all affective Simon experiments that have been conducted until now, participants were asked to respond verbally by saying a positive or negative word. In the present experiment, we used valenced nonverbal responses. As in Experiment 2, positive and negative nouns and adjectives were presented one by one on a computer screen. Before the onset of the word, a manikin appeared above or below the position where the word would be presented. The position of the manikin was determined independently from the grammatical category and valence of the words. Participants could make the manikin run upwards or downwards by pressing one of two keys. They were either instructed to make the manikin run towards nouns and away from adjectives or to make it run towards adjectives and away from nouns. Nothing was mentioned about the valence of the words. The dependent variable was the time that elapsed between the presentation of the word and the first key press. Because it can be assumed that running away (i.e., avoidance or escape) is linked with negative valence whereas running towards (i.e., approach) is linked with positive valence (Cacioppo, Priester, & Berntson, 1993; Lang, 1994; Martin & Levey, 1978), we predicted that participants would need more time to make the manikin run away from positive words and towards negative words than to make it run towards positive words and away from negative words, even though the valence of the words was irrelevant.

Method

Participants.   Thirty-five undergraduates (20 men, 15 women) from various departments at the University of Leuven volunteered to participate.

Materials.   The same words were used as in Experiment 2. All words were written in upper-case letters. The manikin consisted of a circle for the head, a square for the body, and four lines, one for each arm and leg. It was about 1.3 cm high and 0.9 cm wide. Participants could make the manikin move upwards by pressing the key "8" on the numeric part of the keyboard and could make it move downwards by pressing the key "2" on the numeric part of the keyboard. Each time one of these keys was pressed, the manikin moved 20 pixels in the appropriate direction. By alternating the length of the legs each time a key was pressed, it actually appeared as if the manikin walked across the screen. All stimuli were shown on a black background and were presented on a 70 Hz VGA screen connected to an IBM-compatible 386 computer. Presentations were controlled by a Turbo Pascal 5.0 program that operated in graphics mode. The time between the onset of the word and the first key press was measured using a highly accurate Turbo Pascal timer (Bovens & Brysbaert, 1990). Participants were seated in front of the computer screen at a distance of approximately 40 cm.

Procedure.   All participants were tested individually. Instructions that were presented on the computer screen, informed the participants that on each trial they would see a noun or an adjective. There would also be a man-like figure drawn either below or above the word. Their task was to move the manikin towards or away from the word, depending on whether the word was a noun or an adjective. The response assignment was counterbalanced over participants.

The number of practice and experimental trials was the same as in Experiments 1 and 2, as was the way in which trials were randomised. All words were presented in the centre of the computer screen. The manikin was presented in the centre of the upper or lower half of the screen. Whether it appeared in the upper or lower part was determined randomly on each trial. Each practice and experimental trial started with the presentation of the manikin, accompanied by a warning tone (1000 Hz, 200 ms). The word appeared 750 ms after the onset of the manikin. All visual stimuli remained on the screen until the manikin had reached the centre of the screen or had reached the edge of the screen. The next trial was initiated after 1500 ms. Only the first key press after the onset of the word was registered.

Results and discussion

The mean reaction time on congruent (towards positive words; away from negative words) and incongruent (towards negative words; away from positive words) experimental trials was calculated for each participant. Reaction times on trials where an incorrect response was given (7.04% of all trials), were not taken into account. Means are displayed in Table 1.

An a priori F-test showed that the reaction times were significantly shorter on congruent trials than on incongruent trials, $F(1, 34) = 6.00$, $MS_e = 3151.41$, but the number of errors on congruent and incongruent trials did not differ significantly, $F(1, 34) = 2.06$, $MS_e = 4.34$.

The present study provides the first demonstration of an affective Simon effect involving nonverbal responses. The results are also relevant for the hypothesis that stimulus valence is ultimately linked to behavioural approach-avoidance tendencies (Cacioppo et al., 1993; Lang, 1994; Martin & Levey, 1978). Although the responses did not involve an actual approach or avoidance behaviour of the participants themselves, participants did have to make a decision about whether to make an external stimulus (i.e., a manikin) move towards or away from another stimulus (i.e., a positive or negative word). The fact that participants needed more time to make a manikin approach negative words and run away from positive words than to make the manikin approach positive words and run away form negative words shows that the valence of the word biased the decision to make the manikin approach or avoid the word. Given that valenced words can bias decisions regarding the direction of movement of external stimuli, it is likely they can also bias decisions regarding the direction of movement of the individual itself. So one way in which valenced stimuli could predispose individuals to approach or avoid is by biassing the decision with regard to the type of behaviour that needs to be emitted.

GENERAL DISCUSSION

During a Simon task, participants are to process a relevant stimulus feature in order to select the correct response while ignoring an irrelevant feature of the stimulus-display that is meaningfully related to the responses but not to the relevant stimulus feature (De Houwer & Eelen, 1998; Kornblum & Lee, 1995). De Houwer and Eelen (1998) introduced an affective variant of the Simon paradigm in which stimulus-valence is the irrelevant feature and responses have affective properties. Even though they only used words as stimuli and responses, and grammatical category as the relevant feature, they claimed that the affective Simon effect is a general phenomenon that can also be obtained with other stimuli, responses, and relevant features. The present results clearly support this claim. The match between the (irrelevant) valence of the presented stimulus and the valence of the correct response influenced reaction times not only when words were used as stimuli (Experiments 1 and 2), but also when pictures of valenced objects were presented (Experiment 3). Moreover, such affective Simon effects were obtained not only when grammatical category was relevant (Experiment 2) but also when the semantic category (Experiment 1) and letter-case (Experiment 2) of words, and the semantic category of pictures (Experiment 3) was relevant. Finally, the results of Experiment 4 showed that affective Simon effects can also be observed when participants are asked to make non-verbal approach-avoidance responses. As such, the present experiments illustrate the flexibility of the affective Simon task and demonstrate the generalisability of the affective Simon effect. Moreover, they provide additional evidence for the hypothesis that nonverbal stimuli can evoke automatic affective reactions (Experiment 2; also see Hermans et al., 1994) and suggest ways in which valenced stimuli can influence approach-avoidance behaviour in an automatic way (Experiment 4).

Although we thus demonstrated that affective Simon effects can be observed under a variety of conditions, in Experiment 3 we did not find an affective Simon effect when participants had to determine whether a picture was presented in colour or in black and white whereas a clear Simon effect did occur when the semantic category of the depicted object was relevant. Analyses on log-transformed means showed that this difference was not due to an artefact caused by differences in overall reaction times (Chapman et al., 1994). Further research is needed in order to determine why the Simon effect was absent in the perceptual condition of Experiment 3. One can think of a number of explanations. A first and rather uninteresting explanation is that participants in the perceptual condition diverted their eyes away from the picture and thus prevented full processing of the picture at the peripheral level. When diverting their eyes to a certain extent, they might still have been able to determine the colour of the picture but not other characteristics of the picture such as the identity of the depicted object. According to a second account, task difficulty moderates the magnitude of the affective Simon effect. One could, for instance, assume that participants actively try to prevent that their performance would be influenced by the (irrelevant) valence of the stimuli. When the task is easy (e.g., when they have to respond on the basis of a simple perceptual feature such as colour), enough resources might be available to prevent such an influence. However, when the task is difficult (e.g., when the semantic category of the depicted objects is relevant), there might not be enough resources left to block out the effects of the automatic affective processing. A final account is perhaps theoretically the most interesting one. According to this account, the probability that or the extent to which stimuli are automatically processed affectively depends on the cognitive processes and representations that are activated during the task. For instance, some have suggested that semantic representations need to be activated before the valence of a stimulus can be determined (automatically) (see Bower, 1991; De Houwer & Hermans, 1994). The absence of an affective

Simon effect in the perceptual condition of Experiment 3 can be explained on the basis of this account if one assumes that semantic representations are not activated when participants have to process the colour of the pictures.[5] One way to decide between these three accounts is to manipulate the type of feature (semantic vs. nonsemantic) and task difficulty (easy vs. difficult discrimination) in an orthogonal manner, while making sure that participants do not block out stimuli at a peripheral level.

Manuscript received 14 April 1999
Revised manuscript received 19 August 1999

REFERENCES

Bargh, J.A. (1992). The ecology of automaticity. Toward establishing the conditions needed to produce automatic processing effects. *American Journal of Psychology, 105*, 181–199.

Boucart, M., & Humphreys, G.W. (1994). Attention to orientation, size, luminance, and color: Attentional failure within the form domain. *Journal of Experimental Psychology: Learning, Memory, and Cognition, 20*, 61–80.

Bovens, N., & Brysbaert, M. (1990). IBM PC/XT/AT and PS/2 Turbo Pascal timing with extended resolution. *Behavior Research Methods, Instruments, and Computers, 22*, 332–334.

Bower, G.H. (1991). Mood congruity of social judgements. In J.P. Forgas (Ed.), *Emotion and social judgements* (pp. 31–54). Oxford: Pergamon.

Cacioppo, J.T., Priester, J.R., & Berntson, G.G. (1993). Rudimentary determinants of attitudes: II. Arm flexion and extension have differential effects on attitudes. *Journal of Personality and Social Psychology, 65*, 5–17.

Centre for the Study of Emotion and Attention [CSEA-NIMH] (1995). *The international affective picture system: Photographic slides*. Gainsville, FL: The Center for Research in Psychophysiology, University of Florida.

Chapman, L.J., Chapman, J.P., Curran, T.E., & Miller, M.B. (1994). Do children and the elderly show heightened semantic priming? How to answer the question. *Developmental Review, 14*, 159–185.

Craft, J.L., & Simon, J.R. (1970). Processing symbolic information from a visual display: Interference from an irrelevant directional cue. *Journal of Experimental Psychology, 83*, 415–420.

De Houwer, J. (1998). The semantic Simon effect. *Quarterly Journal of Experimental Psychology, 51A*, 683–688.

De Houwer, J. (in preparation). A structural analysis of paradigms used to measure implicit attitudes: What's new?

De Houwer, J., & Eelen, P. (1998). An affective variant of the Simon paradigm. *Cognition and Emotion, 12*, 45–61.

---

[5] One could argue that the third hypothesis is contradicted by the fact that significant affective Simon effects were observed when semantic processing of the stimuli was not necessary, as was the case in the letter-case condition of Experiment 2. However, the fact stimuli do not *have to be* processed semantically does not mean that they *are* not (partially) processed semantically. Processing at the semantic stage may have started at a moment in time when processing at a perceptual stage has not yet been completed (e.g., Boucart & Humphreys, 1994; Humphreys, Riddoch, & Quinlan, 1988; Klopfer, 1996; Seidenberg & McClelland, 1989). Using a semantic variant of the Simon paradigm, De Houwer (1998, Experiment 2) was able to demonstrate that semantic representations are automatically activated when one has to determine the letter-case of words.

De Houwer, J., & Hermans, D. (1994). Differences in the affective processing of words and pictures. *Cognition and Emotion, 8,* 1–20.

Hermans, D., & De Houwer, J. (1994). Affective and subjective familiarity ratings of 740 Dutch words. *Psychologica Belgica, 34,* 115–139.

Hermans, D., De Houwer, J., & Eelen, P. (1994). The affective priming effect: Automatic activation of evaluative information in memory. *Cognition and Emotion, 8,* 515–533.

Humphreys, G.W., Riddoch, M.J., & Quinlan, P.T. (1988). Cascade processes in picture identification. *Cognitive Neuropsychology, 5,* 67–103.

Klopfer, D.S. (1996). Stroop interference and color-word similarity. *Psychological Science, 7,* 150–157.

Kornblum, S., & Lee, J.-W. (1995). Stimulus-Response compatibility with relevant and irrelevant stimulus dimensions that do and do not overlap with the response. *Journal of Experimental Psychology: Human Perception and Performance, 21,* 855–875.

Lang, P.J. (1994). The motivational organization of emotion: Affect-reflex connections. In S.H.M. van Goozen, N.E. Van de Poll, & J.A. Sergeant (Eds.), *Emotions: Essays on emotion theory* (pp. 61–93). Hillsdale, NJ: Erlbaum.

Lang, P.J., Bradley, M.M., & Cuthbert, B.N. (1995). *International affective picture system (IAPS): Technical manual and affective ratings.* Gainesville, FL: The Center for Research in Psycholophysiology, University of Florida.

Levelt, W.J.M. (1989). *Speaking: From intention to articulation.* Cambridge, MA: MIT Press.

Lu, C.-H., & Proctor, R.W. (1995). The influence of irrelevant location information on performance: A review of the Simon and spatial Stroop effects. *Psychonomic Bulletin and Review, 2,* 174–207.

Martin, I., & Levey, A.B. (1978). Evaluative conditioning. *Advances in Behaviour Research and Therapy, 1,* 57–102.

Posner, M.I., & Snyder, C.R.R. (1975). Attention and cognitive control. In R.L. Solso (Ed.), *Information processing and cognition: The Loyola Symposium* (pp. 55–85). Hillsdale, NJ: Erlbaum.

Roelofs, A. (1992). A spreading activation theory of lemma retrieval in speaking. *Cognition, 42,* 107–142.

Seidenberg, M.S., & McClelland, J.L. (1989). A distributed, developmental model of word recognition and naming. *Psychological Review, 96,* 523–568.

Shiffrin, R.M., & Schneider, W. (1977). Controlled and automatic human information processing: II. Perceptual learning, automatic attending, and a general theory. *Psychological Review, 84,* 127–190.

Simon, J.R. (1990). The effects of an irrelevant directional cue on human information processing. In R.W. Proctor & T.G. Reeve (Eds.), *Stimulus-response compatibility: An integrated perspective* (pp. 31–86). Amsterdam: North-Holland.

Simon, J.R., & Rudell, A.P. (1967). Auditory S-R compatibility: The effect of an irrelevant cue on information processing. *Journal of Applied Psychology, 51,* 300–304.

COGNITION AND EMOTION, 2001, *15* (2), 207–230

Using the Implicit Association Test to investigate attitude-behaviour consistency for stigmatised behaviour

Jane E. Swanson

University of Washington, Seattle, USA

Laurie A. Rudman

Rutgers University, New Jersey, USA

Anthony G. Greenwald

University of Washington, Seattle, USA

To consciously bolster behaviour that is disapproved by others (i.e., stigmatised behaviour) people may hold and report a favourable attitude toward the behaviour. However, achieving such bolstering outside awareness may be more difficult. Explicit attitudes were measured with self-report measures, and the Implicit Association Test was used to assess implicit attitudes toward behaviour held by stigmatised actors (smokers) and nonstigmatised actors (vegetarians and omnivores). Smokers' showed greater attitude-behaviour consistency in their explicit attitudes toward smoking that in their implicit attitudes. By contrast, vegetarians and omnivores showed attitude-behaviour-consistency at both implicit and explicit levels. Smokers' implicit negative attitudes toward smoking may reflect its status as a stigmatised behaviour, or its addictive nature.

There are many behaviours that people engage in despite knowing that others regard the behaviour as unwise, objectionable, and possibly immoral. How do the people who engage in such behaviours cognitively adjust to this stigmatised character of their own behaviour? Smoking provides an interesting behaviour to study because of its having changed in recent years from being a socially

Correspondence should be addressed to Jane Swanson or Anthony Greenwald, Department of Psychology, Box 351525, University of Washington, Seattle, WA 98195-1525, USA or to Laurie Rudman, Psychology Department, Tillet Hall, Livingston Campus, Rutgers University, 53 Ave. E., Piscataway, NJ 08854, USA; e-mail: swansonj@u.washington.edu, rudman@rci.rutgers.edu, or agg@u.washington.edu

This research was supported by Grants MH-41328 and MH-001533 from National Institute of Mental Health and by Grant SBR-9710172 from National Science Foundation to the third author.

http://www.tandf.co.uk/journals/pp/02699931.html   DOI:10.1080/0269993004200060

attractive behaviour to being a stigmatised behaviour. At present, laws restrict smokers' behaviour, smokers are viewed as unhealthy, dirty, weak-willed, and morally bereft (Goldstein, 1991; Rozin & Singh, 1998), and the majority of smokers are aware that their habit increases their chances of heart disease, lung cancer, and premature death (Shopland & Brown, 1987). Because this knowledge and the stigma associated with smoking are inconsistent with knowing that they smoke, smokers may experience a dissonance-like tension (Festinger, 1957). This may prompt their creation or modification of cognitions to support their behaviour (cf. Festinger, 1957, pp. 5–6). By contrast, people who engage in nonstigmatised behaviour have no occasion to respond to such inconsistencies.

People with stigmatised occupations (e.g., topless dancers and morticians) may downplay the negative aspects of their professions, emphasising instead the prosocial benefits they provide (Thompson, 1991; Thompson & Harred, 1992). Along these lines, smokers perceive less health-related consequences of smoking than do nonsmokers (Halpern, 1994; Johnson, 1968), even though both groups have the same factual knowledge (McMaster & Lee, 1991; Miller & Slap, 1989). Further, the more smokers acknowledge the health risks of smoking, the more they produce rationalisations for their habit (Johnson, 1968). And, although smokers' self-reported attitudes toward smoking range from neutral to slightly unfavourable, they nevertheless have more positive attitudes toward smoking than do nonsmokers (Chassin, Presson, Sherman & Edwards, 1991; Stacy, Bentler, & Flay, 1994). In sum, the literature suggests that stigmatised actors—including smokers—cognitively bolster their actions in the face of widespread disapproval.

All prior research on smokers' cognitive bolstering of their smoking habit has been conducted using self-report measures. The present research additionally used implicit measures. The primary goal of this research was to determine whether cognitive bolstering of stigmatised behaviour would also be evident on implicit measures. Smoking was an obvious choice for the stigmatised behaviour, and dietary preferences were used as comparison nonstigmatised behaviours. A priori, there was no reason to suspect that smokers' attitudes would be inconsistent at the implicit level. Existing statements of cognitive consistency theories do not address a distinction between implicit and explicit cognitions. Because Greenwald et al. (in press; Greenwald et al., 1999) have reported greater consistency among implicit than explicit cognitions in other domains, there was actually some reason to anticipate that implicit measures might show greater attitude-behaviour consistency than would explicit measures. Nevertheless, when people act in ways that elicit frequent negative feedback from others, inconsistency may be unavoidable at the implicit level. In support of this view, Greenwald et al. (1999) found one exception to their general observation that people who liked themselves and identified with their group also showed ingroup bias. Elderly subjects with high self-esteem implicitly disidentified with their age group, also showing strongly greater implicit preference for young than old. This implicit finding in the age attitude domain may indicate the extent to which old age is stigmatised in American society. Similarly, smokers' implicit cognitions may indicate the extent to which smoking is stigmatised.

The development of implicit measures that are sensitive to individual differences provides the opportunity to examine implicit cognitions associated with stigmatised behaviours. Behaviour-relevant cognitions include attitudes toward the self and toward the behaviour, and association of self with the behaviour. Implicit attitudes are measured by assessing the automatic association between the attitude object and positive or negative valence (Fazio, 1990; Greenwald & Banaji, 1995; Greenwald, McGhee, & Schwartz, 1998—in the emotion literature, this is referred to as automatic affect, e.g., Winkielman, Zajonc, & Schwarz, 1997).[1] Both cognitive and emotion theorists conceptualise implicit cognitions (e.g., attitudes and beliefs) as similar to implicit memory, such that each is revealed when past experience indirectly influences responses "in a fashion not introspectively known by the actor" (Greenwald & Banaji, 1995, p. 4). By contrast, explicit cognitions are presumed to require deliberate retrieval of information.

Evidence from prejudice and stereotype research indicates that implicit and explicit cognitions are only weakly correlated (e.g., Blair, in press; Brauer, Wasel, & Niedenthal, 2000; Greenwald et al., 1998; Rudman, Ashmore, & Gary, 2000); Rudman, Greenwald, Mellott, & Schwartz, 1999). This is not to suggest that these constructs are completely independent or that their relationship cannot be moderated (Rudman et al., 2000; see also Wegner & Bargh, 1998; for a discussion of the interface between implicit and explicit cognitions). However, these findings do suggest that the psychological properties of implicit and explicit cognitions can and do diverge.

The Implicit Association Test

The Implicit Association Test (IAT; Greenwald et al., 1998) is a flexible measure of implicit social cognition, including attitudes, stereotypes, and self-concept (e.g., Greenwald et al., in press; Rudman et al., 2000). The method assumes that performing tasks that oblige people to sort well-associated categories together is easier than performing tasks in which the categories to be grouped together are not associated. For example, the *self-esteem* IAT involves four categories: two contrasted target concept categories (*self* and *other*) and two contrasted attribute categories (*pleasant* and *unpleasant*; see Figure 1). In the data-gathering trial blocks of the IAT, subjects perform two combined cate-

---

[1] Affect can be conceptualised as emotions or as the evaluation attached to a particular (attitude) object (Isen & Diamond, 1989). The present paper is concerned with affect in the latter sense—specifically, attitudes toward one's self and one's behaviour when the behaviour is stigmatised (e.g., smoking) versus when it is nonstigmatised (e.g., vegetarianism).

IAT Items in the Four Categories	SELF me my mine self	OTHER they them their other	PLEASANT cuddle happy smile joy	UNPLEASANT Pain Awful Disaster Grief

	respond left	respond right
Task 1	UNPLEASANT	PLEASANT
Task 2	SELF	OTHER
Task 3	SELF + UNPLEASANT	OTHER + PLEASANT
Task 4	OTHER + UNPLEASANT	SELF + PLEASANT

Figure 1.   Illustration of the Implicit Association Test (IAT). The IAT starts by introducing subjects to the four categories used in the task. In this example, the categories are introduced in Tasks 1 and 2. In Task 1, subjects are asked to respond "left" to *pleasant* words and "right" to *unpleasant* words. In Task 2, subjects respond "left" to *self* words and "right" to *other* words. The IAT measure is obtained by comparing response latencies in the next two tasks, one in which *self* and *unpleasant* are assigned to "left" and *other* and *pleasant* to "right", and another in which *other* and *unpleasant* are assigned to "left" and *self* and *pleasant* are assigned to "right". If the subject responds more rapidly when *self* and *pleasant* share a response, this indicates that the *self-pleasant* association is stronger than the *self-other* association.

gorisation tasks that map the four categories of stimuli (self, other, pleasant and unpleasant) onto two response keys. In one combined task (self+unpleasant), subjects are instructed to rapidly press one key for both *self* and *unpleasant* stimuli and to press another key for both *other* and *pleasant* stimuli. In the second combined task (self+pleasant), both *self* and *pleasant* get one response and both *other* and *unpleasant* get the alternative response. (Order of the two combined tasks is counterbalanced across subjects.) The IAT effect is the difference between latencies for these two combined categorisation tasks. For subjects with high implicit self-esteem, the self+pleasant combined task is expected to be performed substantially more rapidly than the self+unpleasant combined task.

EXPERIMENT 1

In an initial study of smokers' implicit attitudes toward smoking, Experiment 1 contrasted smoking with two different target concepts (sweets or exercise) to create IATs that might discriminate between smokers and nonsmokers, provided smokers' cognitions were consistent with their actions. The choice of contrast categories was based on the hypothesis that nonsmokers should prefer sweets to smoking as an oral gratification, whereas smokers might show a reverse pattern. In addition, nonsmokers should prefer a healthy behaviour (exercise) to an unhealthy behaviour (smoking), whereas smokers might not show a preference. Finally, self-report attitudes toward smoking and either sweets or exercise were assessed for comparison purposes and were expected to discriminate between smokers and nonsmokers.

Method

Subjects.   These were 93 undergraduates at the University of Washington who received course credit for their participation. Subjects who were ex-smokers ($n = 9$) were excluded from all analyses. The final sample consisted of 38 smokers and 46 nonsmokers.

Materials

Explicit measures. Subjects completed a measure that allowed us to classify them as smokers or nonsmokers. Subjects also completed a set of eight semantic differential items for each target concept (smoking and sweets or exercise). Each 7-point item consisted of polar-opposite adjective pairs (*good-bad, healthy-unhealthy, sexy-unsexy, pleasant-unpleasant, harmless-harmful, sociable-unsociable, ugly-glamorous, calming-stressful*). Subjects were instructed to check the middle section if the attribute dimension was irrelevant to the target concept. Composite scores for each target concept (e.g., smoking) were calculated by scoring the 7-pt scale from -3 to $+3$ and summing the ratings given on each adjective pair for a target concept. A difference score that corresponded to the IAT target-concept discrimination was calculated by taking the composite scores for the two target concepts and subtracting one from the other. In each case, high scores reflect more positive attitudes toward smoking (compared to exercise or sweets).

Finally, subjects indicated on a feeling "thermometer" how favourable they felt about each target concept. Each thermometer was labelled in 10 degree increments ranging from 0 to 99. In addition, 0 was labelled as "extremely cold or unfavourable", 50 as "neutral", and 99 as "extremely warm or favourable". Thermometer difference scores that corresponded to each of the IAT target concept discriminations were calculated by taking the thermometer scores for the two target concepts and subtracting one from the other. In each case, high scores reflect more positive attitudes toward smoking (compared to exercise or sweets).

Implicit measures. Subjects completed an IAT measuring implicit attitudes toward smoking. Half the subjects completed an IAT that contrasted smoking with exercise and had the attribute dimension of pleasant versus unpleasant. The other half of the subjects completed a similar IAT that contrasted smoking with sweets. The smoking (e.g., cigarettes, ashtray), exercise (e.g., biking, jogging), and sweets (e.g., candy, cookies) stimuli were generated by the authors. The pleasant and unpleasant attributes were selected from Bellezza, Greenwald, and

Banaji (1986). A complete list of the stimuli used in the three experiments is included in the Appendix.

The IAT was administered on IBM-compatible desktop computers.[2] Subjects responded to the categorisation task by pressing either the "A" key with the left forefinger or the "5" key on the numeric keypad with the right forefinger. Each stimulus was presented in black letters in a light grey rectangle in the centre of the screen. The program randomly selected without replacement items from the stimulus lists while not allowing more than three items in a row that would be answered correctly using the same key. An intertrial interval of 150 ms was used. On each side of the stimulus rectangle were labels to remind subjects of the categories assigned to each key for the current task. If the subject responded correctly, a green circle appeared in a small box directly below the stimulus and the program proceeded to the next trial. If the subject responded incorrectly, a red "X" appeared in the box and remained on the screen along with the stimulus, until the subject responded correctly.

Procedure.   On entering the lab, subjects were assigned to individual booths for the duration of the experiment. Subjects completed the explicit measures and were instructed to place them directly into a box marked "completed questionnaires" to maintain their anonymity. The experimenter then administered the IAT, instructing subjects to respond to the stimuli as quickly and accurately as possible. The IAT task consisted of seven blocks of trials: (1) practice of single categorisation task for the attribute (e.g., unpleasant/pleasant); (2) practice of single categorisation task for the target concept (e.g., smoking/exercise); (3) practice of combined categorisation task (e.g. smoking+unpleasant/exercise+pleasant); (4) critical trials for the block 3 combined categorisation task; (5) practice of single categorisation task for the attribute dimension, but with the response keys reversed from the block 1 assignment; (6) practice of combined categorisation task (e.g., smoking+pleasant/exercise+unpleasant); (7) critical trials for the block 6 categorisation task. Order in which subjects performed the mixed categorisation blocks (i.e., blocks 3–4 and 6–7) was counterbalanced. Each practice block had 20 trials and each critical block had 40 trials. On completion of the computer task, subjects were debriefed and thanked.

Results and discussion

Data reduction.   These procedures were consistent with Greenwald et al. (1998). The first two trials in each block were discarded because these response latencies were typically longer. Trials that had latencies greater than 3000 ms or shorter than 300 ms were recoded to 3000 ms and 300 ms, respectively to control

---

[2] This experiment used the 2/17/97 version of the WinIAT program developed by Shelly Farnham.

for inattention or anticipation. Latencies were log-transformed to meet distributional assumptions for analysis of variance.

Smoking IAT effects. Each subject's smoking IAT effect was calculated by taking the latency for the smoking + unpleasant task minus the latency for the smoking + pleasant task. Thus, more positive scores indicated greater facility for the smoking + pleasant task than the smoking + unpleasant task and were interpreted as more favourable implicit attitudes toward smoking relative to the contrast category (i.e., sweets or exercise). Because the contrast categories did not influence results, $F(1, 83) = 0.23$, $p = .633$, they were combined for the remaining analyses.

If smokers' implicit attitudes are consistent with their behaviour, their IAT effects should be more positive than those of nonsmokers. However, smokers and nonsmokers alike strongly preferred the contrast category over smoking ($Ms = -300$ ms vs. -354 ms, respectively), and their IAT effects did not differ significantly, $F(1, 83) = 0.83$, $p = .366$. By contrast, the explicit measures showed group differences in each case. That is, smokers liked smoking relative to the contrast category more than did nonsmokers, using both the thermometer, $F(1, 82) = 18.52$, $p = 10^{-5}$ and the semantic differential, $F(1, 82) = 10.62$, $p = .002$. These findings suggest that smokers cognitively accommodate their stigmatised behaviour at the explicit, but not implicit, level.

The correlations between the attitude IAT and the explicit measures were significant when the thermometer was used, $r(80) = .30$, $p = .007$, or marginally significant when the semantic differential was used, $r(80) = .21$, $p = .060$. The explicit attitude measures were also related, $r(80) = .52$, $p = 10^{-7}$.

The findings that smokers and nonsmokers have comparably negative implicit attitudes toward smoking, whereas explicit measures discriminated them, suggest that smokers are more successful at bolstering their smoking behaviour at the explicit than implicit level. However, an alternative explanation is that smokers may not implicitly identify themselves with the behaviour. If smokers dissociate themselves from an activity they dislike (as elderly people dissociated from their age group; Greenwald et al., in press), their cognitions could be described as consistent. Thus, Experiment 2 was conducted, in part, to test differences in implicit identification with smoking between smokers and nonsmokers. In addition, Experiment 2 sought to compare the psychological characteristics of stigmatised actors (smokers) and nonstigmatised actors (vegetarians and omnivores).

EXPERIMENT 2

The lack of differences in smokers' and nonsmokers' implicit attitudes in Experiment 1 suggested that smokers engage in a behaviour they do not implicitly like. However, the contrasts used in Experiment 1 were positive for both smokers and nonsmokers (sweets and exercise). One objective of

Experiment 2 was to test implicit attitudes toward smoking using a negative contrast (stealing). In this case, the contrast category is even more stigmatised and less justifiable than the behaviour of interest. We therefore expected smokers and nonsmokers alike to prefer smoking to stealing, but if implicit attitudes for smokers were consistent with their behaviour, we expected smokers to show this preference more so than nonsmokers.

We also examined the extent to which smokers and nonsmokers implicitly identified with smoking versus stealing.[3] We expected smokers to identify more with smoking than with stealing, and to show this identification more than nonsmokers. If smokers showed greater tendency to identify with smoking, but nonetheless possessed implicit attitudes that were similar to those of nonsmokers, the results would suggest that smokers' behaviour-relevant cognitions are indeed inconsistent at the implicit level.

Experiment 2 also examined implicit and explicit attitudes toward vegetarianism, a nonstigmatised behaviour. One objective was to replicate earlier findings indicating attitude-behaviour consistency among vegetarians and omnivores with respect to eating meat versus other sources of protein (Swanson & Greenwald, 1998). The contrasts used were white meat versus other protein. Swanson and Greenwald (1997) showed that white meat was eaten more frequently and liked more (explicitly and implicitly) by omnivores than red meat. The category of other protein contained sources of protein that most lacto-ovo vegetarians use in place of meat (e.g., tofu and nuts). Because vegetarians and omnivores are nonstigmatised actors, we expected each group to show consistent relations between their attitudes toward the foods they ate, identification with their status as vegetarians or omnivores, and their behaviour (see also Rozin, Markwith, & Stoess, 1997). These consistent cognitions could be characterised as, "If I do X, then I identify with X, and X is good" (cf. Heider, 1958). Thus, vegetarians should identify with other proteins and have more favourable attitudes toward other protein (and less favourable attitudes toward meat), compared to omnivores. These predictions were examined using implicit and explicit measures.

Method

Subjects. These were 113 undergraduate psychology students at the University of Washington who received course credit for participation. Subjects who were ex-smokers were excluded from the smoking IAT ($n = 7$), and subjects who were ex-vegetarians were excluded from the vegetarian IAT ($n = 5$). Four subjects were excluded from both IATs on the basis of their latency data (e.g., due to error rates $> 25\%$); in addition, 5 and 3 subjects were excluded from the

---

[3] Past research has shown the IAT to be an effective measure of implicit self-concept and identity (e.g., Farnham, Banaji, & Greenwald, 1999; see also Rudman, Greenwald, & McGhee, in press).

smoking and vegetarian IATs, respectively, for similar reasons. The final sample sizes consisted of 59 nonsmokers, 37 smokers, 66 omnivores, and 34 vegetarians.

Materials and procedure

Explicit measures. Subjects completed a measure that allowed us to classify them as smokers or nonsmokers and as vegetarians or omnivores. They also completed a measure that inquired about their smoking behaviour, including number of cigarettes smoked per day. A similar measure assessed the number of times per year that subjects ate white meat and other sources of protein.

Subjects also completed a set of six semantic differential items for each of the four target concepts (smoking, stealing, white meat, other protein). Each 7-point item consisted of polar-opposite adjective pairs (*beautiful-ugly*, *good-bad*, *pleasant-unpleasant*, *honest-dishonest*, *nice-awful*, and *harmless-harmful*). Subjects were instructed to check the middle section if the attribute dimension was irrelevant to the target concept. Composite scores for each target concept (e.g., smoking) were calculated by scoring the 7-pt scale from -3 to $+3$ and summing the ratings given on each adjective pair for a target concept. Difference scores that correspond to each of the IAT target-concept discriminations were calculated by taking the composite scores for the two target concepts and subtracting one from the other. In each case, high scores reflect more positive attitudes toward smoking (compared to stealing) and toward other protein (compared to white meat).

Finally, subjects indicated on a feeling thermometer how favourable they felt about each of the four target concepts. The feeling thermometer was identical in format to those in Experiment 1 except the range was from 0 to 100. Thermometer difference scores that correspond to each of the IAT target concept discriminations were calculated by taking the thermometer scores for the two target concepts and subtracting one from the other. In each case, high scores reflect more positive attitudes toward smoking (compared to stealing) and toward other protein (compared to white meat).

Implicit measures. Subjects completed a total of four IATs: two implicit attitude IATs and two implicit identification IATs. The two target-concept discriminations used for each type of IAT were smoking versus stealing and white meat versus other protein. Each of these was paired with the attribute dimension of pleasant versus unpleasant to assess attitudes, and with the attribute dimension of self versus other to assess identification.

The self, other, and white meat categories each had three stimuli due to the difficulty of finding items that were good exemplars and known to most people. The three self and three other stimuli consisted of pronouns that referred to self (i.e., me, mine, self) or other (i.e., they, them, other), and that have been used successfully in prior research to measure implicit identification (e.g., Farnham et al., 1999; see also Rudman, Greenwald, & McGhee, in press). The three white meat (chicken, turkey, poultry) and six other protein (e.g., tofu, nuts, cheese) items were from Swanson and Greenwald (1997). The six smoking items (e.g., smoke, cigarette) and the six stealing stimuli (e.g., steal, theft) were generated by the authors. The six pleasant and six unpleasant stimuli were selected from Greenwald et al. (1998). A complete list of the stimuli used in all the experiments is included in the Appendix.

The same procedure was used as in Experiment 1, with the exception that subjects performed two IATs instead of one (IAT order was counterbalanced) and a newer version of the IAT software was used (Farnham, 1997, version 4/17/97).

Results and discussion

Other protein vs. white meat measures.   Each subject's vegetarian attitude IAT effect was calculated by taking the latency for the other protein + unpleasant task minus the latency for the other protein + pleasant task. Thus, more positive scores indicated favourable implicit attitudes towards other protein relative to white meat. An analogous procedure was used to calculate the vegetarian self-concept IAT such that more positive scores indicated stronger identification with other protein than white meat.

It was predicted that vegetarians would have more favourable attitudes toward other protein than meat and identify with other protein more than meat. Omnivores were expected to have more favourable attitudes toward meat than other protein and identify with meat more than other protein. Table 1 reveals that vegetarians preferred other protein to meat ($M = 114$ ms) and omnivores preferred meat to other protein ($M = -70$ ms). Omnivores and vegetarians implicit attitudes were significantly different, $F(1, 76) = 24.03$, $p = 10^{-6}$. The effect size for this difference was large, $d = 1.01$. No other effects emerged, with the exception of an uninterpretable interaction between the procedural variables, IAT effect, and diet, $F(2, 76) = 3.17$, $p = .05$.

Vegetarians also implicitly identified more with other protein than meat ($M = 66$ ms), and omnivores implicitly more with meat than other protein ($M = -46$ ms). Omnivores' and vegetarians' implicit identification with other protein and meat was significantly different, $F(1, 76) = 15.19$, $p = 10^{-4}$, and the effect size for this difference was large, $d = .80$. However, this difference was somewhat qualified by a significant interaction with IAT task order. The differences between omnivores and vegetarians decreased the later the dietary self-concept IAT was presented, $F(2, 76) = 4.14$, $p = .020$.

Both explicit measures indicated that vegetarians preferred other protein to white meat and that omnivores preferred white meat to other protein. The effect sizes for these group differences were large ($ds > 2.00$; see Table 1). In sum, vegetarians and omnivores alike showed cognitive consistency between self-

TABLE 1
Summary statistics for implicit and explicit measures (Experiment 2)

Measure		*Vegetarians* (n = 34)		*Omnivores* (n = 64)		*Difference* Cohen's	
		M	(SD)	M	(SD)	d^a	p^b
Implicit measures							
Other Protein + Pleasant[c]	IAT	113.7	(225.3)	−69.7	(159.8)	1.01	10^{-6}
Other Protein + Me[d]	IAT	66.5	(132.5)	−45.8	(144.4)	.80	10^{-4}
Explicit measures							
Thermometer (prefers other protein)[c]		59.0	(32.5)	1.1	(23.6)	2.18	10^{-17}
Semantic differential (prefers other protein)[c]		15.8	(10.0)	−0.5	(5.1)	2.43	10^{-18}

Measure		*Smokers* (n = 37)		*Nonsmokers* (n = 59)		*Difference* Cohen's	
		M	SD	M	(SD)	d^a	p^b
Implicit measures							
Smoking + Pleasant[c]	IAT	173.0	(112.0)	137.1	(150.1)	.27	.133
Smoking + Me[f]	IAT	140.4	(96.3)	92.8	(124.5)	.42	.003
Explicit measures							
Thermometer (prefers smoking)[c]		40.0	(22.3)	5.7	(11.9)	2.14	10^{-17}
Semantic differential (prefers smoking)[c]		9.5	(6.5)	2.1	(2.4)	1.85	10^{-17}

[a] Effect sizes, *d*, were computed by dividing mean difference scores by their pooled SDs. Conventional small, medium, and large effects for *d* are .2, .5, and .8, respectively.

[b] *p*-values correspond to *F*-tests of the differences between group means for the IAT measures and to *t*-tests of the differences between group means for the thermometer and semantic differential measures.

[c] Higher scores reflect more favourable attitudes toward other protein vs. white meat. Thermometer scale ranges from −100 to 100. Semantic differential scale ranges from −36 to 36.

[d] Higher scores reflect stronger association between the self and other protein than the self and white meat.

[e] Higher scores reflect more favourable attitudes toward smoking vs. stealing. Thermometer scale ranges from −100 to 100. Semantic differential scale ranges from −36 to 36.

[f] Higher scores reflect stronger associations between the self and smoking than the self and stealing.

identification, attitudes, and behaviour at both the implicit and explicit level supporting our predictions for nonstigmatised behaviours.

The top half of Table 2 shows the relationships among implicit and explicit measures for vegetarians (top matrix) and vegetarians and omnivores combined (lower matrix). As can be seen, the relationship between implicit attitudes and identity was positive in both matrices (*r*s > .60). In addition, the lower matrix reveals that implicit and explicit attitude measures were related, as were the

TABLE 2
Correlations among implicit and explicit measures (Experiment 2)

Measures			1	2	3	4	5	6
Other protein vs. white meat comparison								
Implicit measures								
1. Other protein + Pleasant[a]	IAT		—	.65	.28	.31	−.31	.13
2. Other protein + Me[b]	IAT		*.61*	—	.20	.35	−.05	.03
Explicit measures								
3. Thermometer (prefers other protein)[a]			*.54*	*.44*	—	.70	−.57	.28
4. Semantic differential (prefers other protein)[a]			*.51*	*.40*	*.79*	—	−**.46**	.18
5. No. of times/yr eat white meat			−*.30*	−*.37*	−*.54*	−*.50*	—	−.20
6. No. of times/yr eat other protein			**.23**	.09	*.33*	**.21**	.02	—
Smoking vs. stealing comparison								
Implicit measures								
1. Smoking + Pleasant[c]	IAT		—	**.39**	−.15	.04	−.06	
2. Smoking + Me[d]	IAT		*.29*	—	−.03	−.11	.24	
Explicit measures								
3. Thermometer (prefers smoking)[c]			.11	**.24**	—	.73	.08	
4. Semantic differential (prefers smoking)[c]			.09	**.22**	*.81*	—	−.02	
5. No. of cigarettes smoked/day			.14	*.30*	*.60*	*.49*	—	

Bold = $p < .05$. *Italics* = $p < .005$. For the other protein vs. white meat comparison, the lower half of the quadrant contains the correlations for all subjects (*N*s range from 101 to 107) and the upper half contains the correlations for vegetarians (*N*s range from 32 to 34). For the smoking vs. stealing comparison, the lower half of the quadrant contains the correlations for all subjects (*N*s range from 98 to 104) and the upper half of the quadrant contains the correlations for smokers only (*N*s range from 35 to 40).

[a] Attitude measures are scored so more positive scores indicate more favourable attitudes toward other protein relative to white meat.

[b] Identification IAT is scored so more positive scores indicate greater association of self with other protein than self with white meat.

[c] Attitude measures are scores so more positive scores indicate more favourable attitudes toward smoking relative to stealing.

[d] Identification IAT is scored so more positive scores indicate greater association of self with smoking than self with stealing.

implicit identity and explicit attitude measures (with *r*s ranging from .40 to .54). Thus, vegetarians and omnivores showed convergence among implicit and explicit measures of attitude and self-concept. Additionally, self-reported behaviour (frequency of eating white meat and other protein) each correlated in the expected direction with implicit attitudes, implicit identification, and explicit attitudes (i.e., negative for white meat, but positive for other protein).[4] These results show that when behaviours are nonstigmatised, the relations between implicit and explicit measures are robust (Swanson & Greenwald, 1998). Perhaps due to diminished power, the correlations for vegetarians alone (top matrix) were in the expected direction, but only reached significance when measures were matched on method (i.e., the two implicit measures were related, as were several of the explicit measures).

Smoking vs. stealing measures.   Each subject's smoking IAT effect was calculated by taking the latency for the smoking + unpleasant task minus the latency for the smoking + pleasant task. Thus, more positive scores indicated greater facility for the smoking + pleasant task than the smoking + unpleasant task and were interpreted as more favourable implicit attitudes toward smoking relative to stealing. An analogous procedure was used to calculate the smoking self-concept IAT, such that more positive scores indicated stronger identification with smoking than stealing.

Because stealing is more stigmatised than smoking, it was expected that both smokers and nonsmokers would have more favourable attitudes toward smoking than stealing. However, if smokers' implicit attitudes were consistent with their behaviour, they should show this preference more than nonsmokers. Table 1 reveals that both smokers and nonsmokers had more favourable implicit attitudes toward smoking relative to stealing (Ms = 173 ms vs. 137 ms), and that the difference in group means was nonsignificant, $F(1, 72)$ = 2.30, p = .13. Nonetheless, smokers might show consistent behaviour-relevant cognitions if they also disassociated themselves from their habit. However, as expected, smokers' identification with smoking was significantly greater than nonsmokers' identification, Ms = 140 ms vs. 93 ms, $F(1, 72)$ = 9.61, p = .003. The effect size for this difference was larger than the attitude effect size (ds = .42 vs. .27). Because smokers automatically identified with a behaviour more than nonsmokers, but nonetheless did not implicitly like the behaviour more than nonsmokers, their implicit attitudes were inconsistent with their behaviour, as in Experiment 1. By contrast, both explicit measures indicated that smokers preferred smoking over stealing more so than nonsmokers, whose attitudes showed little preference for either behaviour. These differences in smokers' and nonsmokers' explicit attitudes were significant (see Table 1).

The lower half of Table 2 shows the correlations among dependent measures for smokers and nonsmokers (lower matrix) in Experiment 1. The relations between implicit and explicit attitude measures were relatively weak, compared to those for the vegetarians and omnivores (all rs < .15). Nonetheless, implicit identification covaried with implicit and explicit attitude measures, and with

---

[4] Subjects were asked to indicate whether vegetarian or omnivore best represented them. Some self-defined vegetarians (11 out of 34) reported eating white meat infrequently.

self-reported behaviour (number of cigarettes smoked per day), suggesting that greater frequency of smoking was associated with stronger self-identity as a smoker, and generally more positive attitudes. The explicit attitude measures correlated positively with themselves, and with self-reported behaviour. The correlations for smokers alone (upper matrix) were examined for evidence for convergence among implicit and explicit measures. As can be seen, these relations were positive between implicit attitudes and implicit identification, and between the two explicit attitude measures. However, the correlations between implicit and explicit measures were not in the predicted direction and hovered near zero. These results show that when a behaviour is stigmatised (i.e., smoking), the convergence between implicit and explicit measures is relatively weak, compared to when a behaviour is not stigmatised (i.e., dietary preference).

In sum, Experiment 2 replicated Swanson and Greenwald (1998), showing that omnivores and vegetarians have consistent implicit and explicit cognitions associated with the behaviour of eating meat. Omnivores preferred white meat to other protein and identified more with white meat than other protein. Vegetarians preferred other protein to white meat and identified more with other protein than white meat. Experiment 2 also showed that smokers and nonsmokers did not differ in their implicit attitudes toward smoking, although smokers did implicitly identify with smoking more than nonsmokers. In concert with Experiment 1, these findings suggest that smokers' implicit attitudes are inconsistent with their behaviour and self-concept. By contrast, and as in Experiment 1, smokers' explicit attitudes toward smoking were more positive than nonsmokers' attitudes, suggesting that smokers' explicit cognitions are consistent. Taken together, these findings suggest that smokers' cognitive bolstering of their behaviour may be more likely at the explicit than implicit level.

EXPERIMENT 3

Experiment 3 had two goals. The first goal was to test implicit cognitions associated with smoking, using the contrast category of nonsmoking. Advances in IAT technology allowing picture stimuli made using the contrast category of nonsmoking a feasible alternative. Specifically, pictures were taken of common household scenes in which one version had a cigarette and ashtray present. The second version was identical, except for the absence of the cigarette and ashtray. Experiment 3 also examined implicit identification for smokers versus nonsmokers, using pictures in place of semantic stimuli. When contrast categories correspond to the behaviour and its opposite (smoking vs. nonsmoking), people who engage in a behaviour should prefer it to its opposite (e.g., smokers should prefer smoking to nonsmoking) and be identified with it more than its opposite (e.g., smokers should identify more with smoking than nonsmoking). Evidence of consistency among smokers' behaviour-relevant cognitions requires showing that smokers prefer smoking over nonsmoking and showing a difference in smokers' and nonsmokers' attitudes that matches their expected differences in identification with smoking.

The second goal was to test the possibility that smokers might achieve implicitly consistent cognitions by lowering their self-esteem. The pattern of consistent cognitions can be characterised as "If I do X, and I identify with X, and X is bad, then I am also bad". Therefore, it was important to examine whether smokers' self-esteem is lower than nonsmokers. Because past research has shown robust implicit self-esteem for a variety of social groups (Farnham et al., 1999), it was hypothesised that smokers would have equally positive implicit self-esteem as nonsmokers. As a result, any evidence for inconsistency among smokers' behaviour-relevant cognitions would not be attributable to lowered self-esteem.

Method

Subjects.   These were 87 undergraduate psychology students at the University of Washington who received course credit for participation. Of these subjects, 53 were self-reported nonsmokers and 43 were self-reported smokers. A total of 21 subjects (12 nonsmokers and 9 smokers) were excluded from all analyses for technical reasons (e.g., high error rates).[5] The similarity between the smoking and nonsmoking pictures was higher than what is generally found between the target contrast stimuli and may have led to the observed high error rates. The final sample consisted of 35 smokers and 41 nonsmokers.

Materials and procedure
Explicit measures. Smoking behaviour was assessed as in Experiment 2. Attitudes toward smoking were assessed similarly as in Experiment 1, with the exception that only a single feeling thermometer and a single semantic differential were used (each were labelled "Smoking"). Self-esteem was measured using the Rosenberg Self-Esteem Scale (Rosenberg, 1979) and a feeling thermometer measure (labelled "Yourself").

Implicit measures. Subjects completed three IATs that assessed attitudes toward smoking, identification with smoking, and implicit self-esteem. In the attitude and identification IATs, the target concepts were smoking versus non-smoking. Eight pairs of pictures were used to represent these concepts. Smoking versus nonsmoking pictures varied only in the presence versus absence of a cigarette and ashtray. The settings were common domestic situations in which one might smoke (e.g., reading the newspaper at a table; see Appendix). The

---

[5] Examination of the practice block distinguishing smoking and nonsmoking pictures indicated that smokers and nonsmokers performed equally well (both in terms of latency and errors) at this discrimination. Additionally, all analyses reported in the results section were repeated with these subjects included, and showed no change in the pattern of results presented herein.

attitude IAT paired these pictures with words that were pleasant or unpleasant in meaning. The identification IAT paired these pictures with self versus other words. The self-esteem IAT used the same self versus other words, paired with the pleasant and unpleasant words used in the attitude IAT (see Appendix).

The procedure was identical to that of Experiment 2 with three exceptions. First, the IATs were administered using a software program that allows both pictures and words to be used as stimuli.[6] Second, subjects performed three IATs (IAT order was counterbalanced). Third, the IAT practice blocks that familiarised subjects with the stimuli differed from Experiment 2. Rather than do single categorisation practice blocks at the start of each IAT task, subjects did five initial blocks to practice the following discriminations (in the order listed): (1) smoking/nonsmoking pictures from pleasant/unpleasant words; (2) pleasant/unpleasant words from self/other words; (3) pleasant from unpleasant words; (4) self from other words; and (5) smoking from nonsmoking pictures. Subjects then completed the mixed categorisation tasks (e.g., smoking + unpleasant/nonsmoking + pleasant) for the three IATs as in Experiment 2 (one practice block and one critical block per task).

Results and discussion

Subject's attitude and self-concept IAT effects were calculated as in Experiment 2. In each case, positive scores indicate more favourable attitudes toward, and identification with, smoking compared to nonsmoking. The self-esteem IAT was scored such that more positive scores indicate more favourable than unfavourable attitudes toward the self. No differences due to procedural variables were found; therefore, the analyses reported below do not include them.

Smoking vs. nonsmoking measures. Table 3 shows the results of Experiment 3's implicit and explicit measures. As can be seen, smokers' implicit attitudes revealed a preference for nonsmoking over smoking ($M = -69$ ms), even though they identified with smoking more than nonsmoking ($M = 125$ ms). In contrast, nonsmokers' implicit attitudes showed a strong preference for nonsmoking over smoking ($M = -245$ ms), and they identified with nonsmoking more than smoking ($M = -20$ ms). Consistent with Experiment 2, this pattern shows more inconsistent implicit cognitions for smokers than nonsmokers that is due to smokers having attitudes inconsistent with their behaviour and their self-concept. Table 3 also reveals that smokers' implicit self-esteem ($M = 322$ ms) was as positive as nonsmokers' implicit self-esteem ($M = 330$ ms). Thus, smokers did not achieve consistency among their behaviour-relevant cognitions via low self-esteem.

---

[6] The program was *Inquisit*, written by Sean Draine (Draine, 1998).

TABLE 3
Summary statistics for implicit and explicit measures (Experiment 3)

Measure		Smokers (n=35)		Nonsmokers (n=41)		Difference Cohen's	
		M	(SD)	M	(SD)	d[a]	p[b]
Implicit measures							
Smoking + Pleasant	IAT[c]	−69.4	(244.9)	−245.3	(257.8)	.70	.008
Smoking + Me	IAT[d]	125.3	(228.5)	−20.1	(192.1)	.71	.002
Me + Pleasant	IAT[e]	322.2	(175.9)	329.5	(143.2)	−.04	.371
Explicit measures							
Smoking thermometer[f]		45.3	(23.7)	16.9	(17.9)	1.36	10^{-7}
Smoking semantic differential[g]		−7.7	(5.6)	−13.5	(3.3)	1.33	10^{-7}
Self thermometer[h]		82.7	(13.1)	84.2	(13.4)	−.08	.630
Rosenberg Self-Esteem Scale[i]		23.5	(5.6)	24.2	(4.7)	−.14	.610

[a] The effect size measure, d was computed by dividing mean differences by their pooled SDs. Conventional small, medium, and large effects for d are .2, .5, and .8, respectively.
[b] p-values correspond to t-tests of the differences between smokers and nonsmokers.
[c] Higher scores reflect more favourable attitudes toward smoking vs. nonsmoking.
[d] Higher scores reflect stronger association between self and smoking than self and nonsmoking.
[e] Higher scores reflect more favourable attitudes toward self vs. other.
[f] Higher scores reflect more favourable attitudes toward smoking. Scale ranges from 0 to 100 with 50 being neutral.
[g] Higher scores reflect more favourable attitudes toward smoking. Scale ranges from −18 to 18 with 0 being neutral.
[h] Higher scores reflect higher self-esteem. Scale ranges from 0 to 100 with 50 being neutral.
[i] Higher scores reflect higher self-esteem. Scale ranges from 0 to 30 with 15 being neutral.

Table 3 also shows that using picture stimuli to operationalise a contrast between smoking and nonsmoking enhanced the ability of the attitude IAT to discriminate between smokers and nonsmokers, $t(74) = 2.73$, $p = .008$. The effect size for this difference was moderately large ($d = .70$). This finding suggests that nonsmoking may be the most appropriate contrast to use when assessing implicit attitudes toward smoking, compared to contrasts that are positive for both groups (e.g., exercise) or negative for both groups (e.g., stealing). Consistent with Experiment 2, the identification IAT continued to discriminate between these groups, despite the substitution of picture stimuli for words, $t(74) = −3.17$, $p = .002$. The effect size for this difference was comparable to that shown in Experiment 2 ($d = .71$). Thus, the change in stimulus mode appears to have improved attitude assessment without diminishing self-concept assessment.

The thermometer and semantic differential measures continued to discriminate between smokers and nonsmokers, as in Experiments 1 and 2 (see Table 3). Nonetheless, when a single attitude object was used (''smoking''), smokers' attitudes were, on average, neutral to somewhat unfavourable, albeit more positive than nonsmokers. These findings are consistent with prior research (Chassin et al., 1991; Stacy et al., 1994) and suggest that smokers may bolster their behaviour by viewing their habit somewhat favourably, compared with nonsmokers. Finally, smokers' and nonsmokers' explicit self-esteem were comparable, as assessed by a self (feeling) thermometer and the Rosenberg Self-Esteem Scale (see Table 3), again showing that smokers did not achieve consistency by lowering their self-esteem.

Table 4 shows the relationships among Experiment 3's dependent measures, for smokers and nonsmokers combined (lower matrix) and for smokers only (upper matrix). Replicating Experiment 2, the lower matrix shows covariation between the attitude and self-concept IATs, and implicit self-concept was positively correlated with the explicit attitude measures and self-reported behaviour (number of cigarettes smoked per day). As in Experiment 2, the explicit attitude measures also covaried and were each related to self-reported behaviour. In addition, the attitude IAT was positively related to each explicit attitude measure. However, the upper matrix shows that for smokers alone, the relations between implicit measures were attenuated. As can be seen, only the two explicit attitude measures and two explicit self-esteem measures reliably covaried. Finally, the implicit and explicit self-esteem measures were negligibly related to any of Experiment 3's primary dependent measures (attitudes, self-concept, and self-reported behaviour). The lack of relationship between the implicit and explicit self-esteem measures is consistent with past research showing that the two constructs are independent (Farnham et al., 1999).

In sum, Experiment 3 provided additional evidence that smokers' implicit behaviour-relevant cognitions are inconsistent. At the implicit level, smokers had positive self-esteem, identified more with smoking than nonsmoking, but preferred nonsmoking over smoking. By contrast, nonsmokers had positive self-esteem, identified with nonsmoking more than smoking, and preferred nonsmoking over smoking. These data suggest that smokers are more likely to have implicit attitudes that are inconsistent with their behaviour than nonsmokers. Additionally, Experiment 3 suggested that smokers may explicitly bolster their habit by viewing their behaviour more favourably than nonsmokers do (i.e., as somewhat neutral rather than negative).

GENERAL DISCUSSION

As performers of a stigmatised behaviour, smokers have been observed to consciously reconcile their performance of the behaviour with their negative knowledge concerning it (Chassin et al., 1991; Halpern, 1994; Johnson, 1968). However, because smokers regularly and frequently confront laws that restrict their behaviour, disapproval from others, and information campaigns about smoking's adverse effects, it is possible that they may not be able to resolve this inconsistency at the implicit level.

TABLE 4
Correlations among implicit and explicit measures (Experiment 3)

Measure		Implicit measures			Explicit measures				
		1	2	3	4	5	6	7	8
Implicit measures									
1. Smoking + Pleasant	IAT	—	.31	.00	.27	.16	-.09	.07	.12
2. Smoking + Me	IAT	.34	—	.21	.27	.00	-.13	-.09	.32
3. Me + Pleasant	IAT	-.04	.09	—	.16	.14	.22	.10	.19
Explicit measures									
4. Smoking thermometer		**.32**	**.31**	.01	—	.56	.28	.29	-.10
5. Smoking semantic differential		**.26**	**.23**	.01	.72	—	.02	-.01	.13
6. Self thermometer		-.05	-.14	.19	-.04	-.04	—	**.46**	-.29
7. Rosenberg Self-Esteem Scale		.01	-.02	.07	-.05	.15	.45	—	-.29
8. No. of cigarettes smoked/day		**.29**	.42	.02	.45	.52	-.16	-.14	—

Bold = $p < .05$. *Italics* = $p < .005$. Measures are scored so more positive scores indicate a higher level of the construct being measured. The lower half of the quadrant contains the correlations for all subjects (Ns range from 70 to 76) and the upper half of the quadrant contains the correlations for smokers only (Ns range from 33 to 35).

The results of three experiments were consistent with this view. In Experiments 1 and 2, smokers' implicit attitudes towards smoking were similar to those of nonsmokers, and in Experiment 3 smokers showed greater implicit preference for nonsmoking than smoking. Moreover, in Experiments 2 and 3, smokers strongly identified with a behaviour they did not implicitly like, even though they showed high self-esteem. The pattern of implicit inconsistency for smokers can be characterised as "I am good, and I identify with smoking, but smoking is bad". By contrast, the pattern of smokers' explicit cognitions can be described as, "I am good, and I identify with smoking, and smoking is not so bad".

To obtain comparison data for performers of nonstigmatised actions, Experiment 2 assessed behaviour-relevant cognitions for vegetarians and omnivores. The results clearly showed consistent cognitions for vegetarians and omnivores. Each group identified with their diet, and showed positive attitudes toward the foods they ate, at both the implicit and explicit level. These results are consistent with viewing nonstigmatised behaviours as ones that do not create dissonant implicit or explicit structures.

These findings do not oblige concluding that smokers suffer more from cognitive dissonance than do vegetarians, omnivores, or nonsmokers. It is possible that the experience of cognitive discomfort requires conscious awareness of an inconsistency. Therefore, having inconsistent implicit cognitions may not produce discomfort unless they are brought to people's attention. Future research should examine whether apprising smokers of their incongruent implicit cognitions might facilitate their ability to quit smoking, through dissonance arousal and self-regulatory processes (see Devine & Monteith, 1993, for a review of similar research in the prejudice reduction domain, and see Stone et al., 1994, for relevant research concerning nonperformed-but-admired behaviour).

The behaviours of smoking and vegetarianism were selected because they differ in their level of stigmatisation. Stigmatisation, however, reflects a variety of dimensions (e.g., healthiness, normative pressures, potential for addiction)—any one (or more) of which may cause the observed differences in cognitive consistency. Indeed, while the addictive nature of smoking may contribute to its disapproved of status, it also makes it difficult to eliminate dissonance by abstaining from the behaviour. It is well known that smokers find it difficult to quit smoking (Hellman, Cummings, Haughey, Zielezny, & O'Shea, 1991; Rose, Chassin, Presson, & Sherman, 1996). Thus, the addictive element of smoking may be one reason why smokers might accommodate their behaviour rather than quit smoking. However, the addictive nature of smoking, the most common reason given by smokers for smoking, may also serve to alleviate dissonance by providing a consonant cognition (Festinger, 1957). This cognition effectively dictates to the smoker that "It's out of my control", thus removing any free will or intent on the part of the smoker.

Relationship between implicit and explicit measures

The majority of research using implicit measures has focused on assessing stereotypes and prejudice. For the most part, the relationship between implicit and explicit measures of affect and beliefs toward various social groups is weak (Brauer et al., 2000). A suggested interpretation of this partial dissociation is that self-report measures are more subject to contamination from self-presentation concerns and/or that respondents' unconscious cognitions are, by definition, inaccessible (Dovidio & Fazio, 1992; Greenwald & Banaji, 1995). The present research focused on behaviours and attitudes that are stigmatised (in the case of smokers) and nonstigmatised (in the case of vegetarians' and omnivores' diets). The results of Experiments 2 and 3 showed that smokers' implicit and explicit attitudes were weakly related. By contrast, the results of Experiment 2 showed that vegetarians and omnivores' implicit and explicit attitudes were moderately or strongly related. These findings suggest that the relationship between implicit and explicit measures can be moderated—in the present research, by differences in the stigmatisation of the behaviour. The explicit-implicit link may be stronger for dietary attitudes because they are less subject to the need for cognitive accommodation (as is the case for smokers). Future research should continue to search for moderators of implicit and explicit relations, and to identify the processes by which conscious and unconscious attitudes are driven apart or brought into convergence (cf. Rudman et al., 2000).

Manuscript received 12 May 1999
Revised manuscript received 10 November 1999

REFERENCES

Belleza, F.S., Greenwald, A.G., & Banaji, M.R. (1986). Words high and low in pleasantness as rated by male and female college students. *Behavior Research Methods, Instruments, and Computers, 18*, 299–303.

Blair, I.V. (in press). Implicit stereotypes and prejudice. In G. Moskowitz (Ed.), *Future directions in social cognition.*

Brauer, M., Wasel, W., & Niedenthal, P. (2000). Implicit and explicit components of prejudice. *Review of General Psychology, 4*, 79–101.

Chassin, L., Presson, C.C., Sherman, S.J., Edwards, D.A. (1991). Four pathways to young-adult smoking status: Adolescent social-psychological antecedents in a Midwestern community sample. *Health Psychology, 10*, 409–418.

Devine, P.G., & Monteith, M.J. (1993). The role of discrepancy-associated affect in prejudice. In D.M. Mackie & D.L. Hamilton (Eds.), *Affect, cognition, and stereotyping: Interactive processes in group perception* (pp. 317–344). New York: Academic Press.

Dovidio, J.F., & Fazio, R.H. (1992). New technologies for the direct and indirect assessment of attitudes. In J.M. Tanur (Ed.), *Questions about questions: Inquiries into the cognitive bases of surveys* (pp. 204–237). New York, Russell Sage Foundation.

Draine, S. (1998). *Inquisit* [Computer softwarer]. Seattle, WA: Millisecond Software. Available: *http://www.millisecond.com/*[version 25].

Farnham, S.D. (1997). *FIAT for Windows* [Computer software]. Seattle, WA: Author. Available: http://weber.u.washington.edu/~sfarnham/IAT/[2/17/97 & 4/13/97].

Farnham, S.D., Banaji, M.R., & Greenwald, A.G. (1999). Implicit self-esteem. In D. Abrams & M.A. Hogg, (Eds.), *Social identity and social cognition* (pp. 230–248). Malden, MA: Blackwell.

Fazio, R.H. (1990). Multiple processes by which attitudes guide behavior: The MODE model as an integrative framework. In M.P. Zanna (Ed.), *Advances in experimental social psychology* (Vol. 23, pp. 75–109). New York: Academic Press.

Festinger, L. (1957). *A theory of cognitive dissonance.* Palo Alto, CA: Stanford University Press.

Goldstein, J. (1991). The stigmatization of smokers: An empirical investigation. *Journal of Drug Education, 21*, 167–182.

Greenwald, A.G., & Banaji, M.R. (1995). Implicit social cognition: Attitudes, self-esteem, and stereotypes. *Psychological Review, 102*, 4–27.

Greenwald, A.G., Banaji, M.R., Rudman, L.A., Farnham, S.D., Nosek, B.A., & Mellott, D.S. (1999). *Unified theory of implicit social cognition: Attitudes, stereotypes, and self-concept.* Manuscript submitted for publication.

Greenwald, A.G., Banaji, M.R., Rudman, L.A., Farnham, S.D., Nosek, B.A., & Rosier, M. (in press). Prologue to a unified theory of attitudes, stereotypes, and self-concept. In J.P. Forgas (Ed.), *Feeling and thinking: The role of affect in social cognition and behavior.* New York: Cambridge University Press.

Greenwald, A.G., McGhee, D.E., & Schwartz, J.L.K. (1998). Measuring individual differences in implicit cognition: The Implicit Association Test. *Journal of Personality and Social Psychology, 74*, 1464–1480.

Halpern, M.T. (1994). Effect of smoking characteristics on cognitive dissonance in current and former smokers. *Addictive Behaviors, 19*, 209–217.

Heider, F. (1958). *The psychology of interpersonal relations.* New York: Wiley.

Hellman, R., Cummings, K.M., Haughey, B.P., Zielezny, M.A., & O'Shea, R.M. (1991). Predictors of attempting and succeeding at smoking cessation. *Health Education Research, 6*, 77–86.

Isen, A.M., & Diamond, G.A. (1989). Affect and automaticity. In J.S. Uleman & J.A. Bargh (Eds.), *Unintended thought* (pp. 124–152). New York: Guilford Press.

Johnson, R.E. (1968). Smoking and the reduction of cognitive dissonance. *Journal of Personality and Social Psychology, 9*, 260–265.

McMaster, C. & Lee, C. (1991). Cognitive dissonance in tobacco smokers. *Addictive Behaviors, 16*, 349–353.

Miller, S.K., & Slap, G.B. (1989). Adolescent smoking: A review of prevalence and prevention. *Journal of Adolescent Health Care, 10*, 129–135.

Rose, J.S., Chassin, L., Presson, C.C., & Sherman, S.J. (1996). Prospective predictors of quit attempts and smoking cessation in young adults. *Health Psychology, 15*, 261–268.

Rosenberg, M. (1979). *Conceiving the self.* New York: Basic Books.

Rozin, P., Markwith, M., & Stoess, C. (1997). Moralization and becoming a vegetarian: The transformation of preferences into values and the recruitment of disgust. *Psychological Science, 8*, 67–73.

Rozin, P. & Singh, L. (1998). *The moralization of cigarette smoking in the United States.* Unpublished manuscript, University of Pennsylvannia.

Rudman, L.A., Ashmore, R.D., & Gary, M. (2000). *Unlearning automatic biases: The malleability of implicit stereotypes and prejudice.* Manuscript submitted for publication.

Rudman, L.A., Greenwald, A.G., & McGhee, D.E. (in press). Implicit self-concept and evaluative implicit gender stereotypes: Self and ingroup share desirable traits. *Personality and Social Psychology Bulletin.*

Rudman, L.A., Greenwald, A.G., Mellott, D.S., & Schwartz, J.L.K. (1999). Measuring the automatic components of prejudice: Flexibility and generality of the Implicit Association Test. *Social Cognition, 17*, 1–29.

Shopland, D.R., & Brown, C. (1987). Toward the 1990 objectives for smoking: Measuring the progress with 1985 NHIS data. *Public Health Reports, 102,* 68–73.

Stacy, A.W., Bentler, P.M., & Flay, B.R. (1994). Attitudes and health behavior in diverse populations: Drunk driving, alcohol use, binge eating, marijuana use, and cigarette use. *Health Psychology, 13,* 73–85.

Stone, J., Aronson, E., Crain, A., Winslow, M.P., et al. (1994). Inducing hypocrisy as a means of encouraging young adults to use condoms. *Personality and Social Psychology Bulletin, 20,* 116–128.

Swanson, J.E., & Greenwald, A.G. (1998, May). *Do implicit attitudes and implicit self-concept discriminate between omnivores and vegetarians? Validating the Implicit Association Test.* Paper presented at meetings of the Midwestern Psychological Association, Chicago, IL.

Swanson, J.E., & Greenwald, A.G. (1997). [*Measuring omnivores' implicit attitudes toward different foods*]. Unpublished raw data.

Thompson, W.E. (1991). Handling the stigma of handling the dead: Morticians and funeral directors. *Deviant Behavior, 12,* 403–429.

Thompson, W.E. & Harred, J.L. (1992). Topless dancers: Managing stigma in a deviant occupation. *Deviant Behavior, 13,* 291–311.

Wegner, D.M., & Bargh, J.A. (1998). Control and automaticity in social life. In D.T. Gilbert, S.T. Fiske, & G. Lindzey (Eds.), *The handbook of social psychology* (Vol. 1, pp. 446–496). New York: Oxford University Press.

Winkielman, P., Zajonc, R.B., & Schwartz, M. (1997). Subliminal affect priming resists attributional interventions. *Cognition and Emotion, 11,* 433–465.

APPENDIX

Target concepts and stimuli

Experiment 1

smoking cigarettes, ashtray, tobacco, pipe, smoking, cigars, nicotine, Camels, smokers, Marlboro
exercise jog, run, swim, biking, sports, tennis, diving, gymnastics, workout, aerobics
sweets candy, cookies, cake, pie, pastry, icecream, chocolate, dessert, fudge, sugar

pleasant caress, gold, joy, kindness, peace, success, sunrise, talent, triumph, warmth
unpleasant abuse, assault, brutal, junk, war, failure, filth, bad, slime, vomit

Experiment 2

white meat chicken, turkey, poultry, chicken, turkey, poultry
other protein nuts, grains, tofu, cheese, soybean, yogurt

smoking smoke, cigarette, tobacco, smokers, nicotine, ligher
stealing steal, theft, gun, mugged, robbery, thief

pleasant peace, paradise, joy, love, cuddle, pleasure
unpleasant disaster, divorce, crash, grief, tragedy, agony

self me, mine, self, me, mine, self
other they, them, other, they, them, other

Experiment 3

Scenes used in smoking and nonsmoking pictures: Besides table with lamp and clock-radio, End-table with lamp and book open-faced down, Kitchen table with newspaper spread open and a coffee mug, Two glasses of water at an outdoor table with chairs, Male smoking cigarette on back door-stoop, Bathroom sink, Back doorstoop with BBQ and glass of juice, Computer on desk.

pleasant cuddle, happy, smile, joy, warmth, peace, paradise, love
unpleasant pain, awful, disaster, grief, agony, brutal, tragedy, bad

self me, mine, self, my, me, mine, self, my
other they, them, their, other, they, them, their, other

COGNITION AND EMOTION, 2001, *15* (2), 231–248

Automatic attention to stimuli signalling chances and dangers: Moderating effects of positive and negative goal and action contexts

Klaus Rothermund

University of Trier, Germany

Dirk Wentura

University of Münster, Germany

Peter M. Bak

University of Trier, Germany

Current research on automatic attention allocation focuses on the questions whether there is an asymmetry in attentional biases towards negative and positive stimuli and whether these attentional biases are influenced by situational variables. In an experiment with $N = 48$ participants, automatic allocation of attention to chance and danger stimuli was investigated. Attentional capture was generally larger for chance stimuli than for danger stimuli. Additionally, attentional bias was influenced by the outcome focus of the actual goal orientation. Results revealed an incongruence effect of goal orientation on attentional biases: Attentional capture for the chance and danger stimuli was comparatively stronger when an outcome focus of opposite valence had been induced.

Automatic allocation of attention to negatively or positively valent stimuli is a central topic in social cognition research. Different experiments have revealed that valent stimuli automatically attract attention (see, e.g., Hansen & Hansen, 1988; Pratto, 1994; Pratto & John, 1991; Rothermund, Wentura, & Bak, 1996; Wentura, Rothermund, & Bak, 2000). It is commonly assumed that this attentional bias towards valent stimuli reflects the operation of a global screening mechanism which directs attention to information that is of general importance for the organism. A fast and efficient screening mechanism must rely on a small

Correspondence should be addressed to Klaus Rothermund, Universität Trier, Fachbereich I - Psychologie, D-54286 Trier, Germany; e-mail: rothermu@uni-trier.de

This research was supported by a grant from the research fund of Rheinland-Pfalz, Germany, to Klaus Rothermund and Peter M. Bak.

http://www.tandf.co.uk/journals/pp/02699931.html   DOI:10.1080/0269993004200079

number of important but easily detectable stimulus characteristics. Valence meets these requirements because it can be identified without deeper conscious processing (e.g., Draine & Greenwald, 1998; Greenwald, Draine, & Abrams, 1996; Murphy & Zajonc, 1993; Zajonc, 1980) and is of prime importance for the regulation of action (e.g., for the selection and elicitation of behavioural tendencies like approach or avoidance; Bargh, 1997; Brendl, 1997; Cacioppo, Priester, & Berntson, 1993; Chen & Bargh, 1999; Solarz, 1960; Wentura et al., 2000).

An important question with regard to the functioning of the global affective screening mechanism is whether attention is allocated preferably to positive or to negative information. A closely related question is whether such a possible asymmetry reflects stable parameter settings of the affective attentional system or whether it is influenced by situational and personal variables. Some researchers have argued for a stable attentional bias in favour of negative stimuli. Because warding off dangers is generally more important for the survival of an organism than making use of opportunities or chances, negative stimuli should attract more attention than positive stimuli (see, e.g., Hansen & Hansen, 1988, 1994; Kahneman & Tversky, 1984; Peeters & Czapinski, 1990; Pratto & John, 1991). In accordance with this hypothesis, Pratto and John (1991; see also Pratto, 1994) showed that negative personality trait words produce larger interference effects in a colour-naming task than do positive adjectives.

Other studies do not support the hypothesis of a global attentional bias towards negative information. Wentura et al. (2000; see also Rothermund, Wentura, & Bak, 1995, 1996) found interference of negative *and* positive stimuli in the colour-naming task but these effects were restricted to information that is relevant for the regulation of behaviour, that is, interference effects were observed for adjectives referring to attributes that have unconditionally negative or positive consequences for the traitholder's social environment (e.g., "friendly" or "aggressive"), but not for attributes that are unconditionally positive or negative for the traitholder him/herself (e.g., "happy" or "sad"; see Peeters & Czapinski, 1990). A second line of evidence suggests that attentional bias is influenced by personal variables as well. Inter-individual differences in automatic affective information processing can be found in studies in which attentional biases were investigated in different clinical populations (for a review see Williams, Watts, MacLeod, & Mathews, 1997). Participants with clinical symptoms differ markedly from the nonclinical groups in different parameters of automatic attention allocation (direction and strength of effects). In addition, the pattern of results for the nonclinical control groups of these experiments is rather heterogeneous and does not correspond to the hypothesis of a simple attentional asymmetry towards negative stimuli (see Wentura et al., 2000). Further evidence for the hypothesis of a variable configuration of attentional parameters comes from research on the influence of mood states on automatic affective information processing. In a series of experiments Derryberry (1988, 1989, 1993) could show that giving positive or negative performance feedback in a reaction time task produces characteristic alterations in the processing of valent stimuli. Derryberry (1993) identified three different types of effects that transient mood states can exert on affective information processing: *Focusing* effects reflect an increase in attention for all kinds of relevant stimuli after negative feedback, *congruence* effects reflect an increase in attention for stimuli that correspond to the valence of the previous feedback, and *incongruence* effects reflect the opposite relation. Although the pattern of effects within and across experiments is highly complex and sometimes difficult to interpret, Derryberry's findings demonstrate that the parameters of automatic affective processing are not invariant but are susceptible to the actual mood of a person.

How can this seemingly inconsistent pattern of effects across experiments and subject groups be explained? We want to argue that an adequate understanding of these results can only be gained by analysing the role of automatic attention allocation in a broader functional context. Attentional processes are located at the interface of emotion/motivation and cognition (Derryberry & Tucker, 1994). The key function of automatic attention allocation is to mediate influences of goals, emotions, moods, and task demands on information processing. Not surprisingly, then, processing of valent stimuli is an important aspect of theories of goal pursuit and emotion regulation (e.g., Brandtstädter & Rothermund, in press; Brandtstädter, Wentura, & Rothermund, 1999; Gollwitzer & Moskowitz, 1996; Higgins, 1996; Markus & Nurius, 1986). All of these models specify variables related to motivational processes that differentially influence attentional biases towards or cognitive accessibility of positive and negative information. For instance, goals can be defined in terms of obtaining positive or avoiding negative outcomes (trying to keep one's job vs. trying not to lose it), that is, they are related to a positive or negative *outcome focus* (Higgins, 1996). A similar distinction can be made for the instrumental activities that are used to reach a given goal (trying to make a profitable investment vs. trying to avoid a failure). It is plausible to assume that automatic attention to positive and negative stimuli is influenced by the actual outcome focus of the current goal or activity. Achievement of positive outcomes is fostered by an increased general sensitivity to stimuli signalling opportunities and chances whereas an avoidance of negative outcomes should be accompanied by an attentional bias towards danger signals. From a theoretical point of view, it is important to note that a certain goal or type of task is not linked to a fixed outcome focus. Rather, a positive or negative outcome focus can be induced by external factors (Brendl, Higgins, & Lemm, 1995; Higgins, 1996) or as a function of different phases of goal pursuit (e.g., Brandtstädter et al., 1999; Taylor & Gollwitzer, 1995) and thus may change during the pursuit of a goal or performing a task. Efficient action regulation or goal pursuit is characterised by a shifting between positive and negative attentional foci. It can even be stated that a switching of the outcome focus is a functional sign of goal pursuit. A fixed orientation towards either positive or negative outcomes can be taken as a symptom of an inefficiently rigid and sometimes even pathological action regulation (Markus & Ruvolo, 1989; Williams et al., 1997).

A heterogeneous pattern of findings with regard to attentional biases towards positive or negative information is thus just what one should expect when processes of attention and automatic vigilance are seen as a mediator of motivational influences on cognitive processes. Of course, a mixed pattern of effects alone cannot be taken as sufficient evidence for the proposed hypothesis that motivational influences on information processing are mediated by a flexible adjustment of the parameters of automatic attention allocation. To support this claim, a much more detailed and systematic analysis of the relationship between motivational variables and parameters of the attentional system is needed. In the present article, we will try to take a step further towards such an analysis. In the following experiment, we will focus on the influence of positively and negatively defined goal and action contexts on general automatic vigilance for chance and danger stimuli. For this purpose, attentional bias towards these stimuli in different goal and action contexts shall be compared.

Before we report the procedural details of the experiment, we want to draw some attention to two important methodological aspects of our analysis. The investigation is concerned with *automatic* attentional biases towards positive and negative stimuli *in general*. These specifications imply some restrictions with regard to the measuring of the attentional bias effects. (1) An important criterion for the automatic nature of the processes that produce an effect is that the effect occurs despite an intention to suppress it (e.g., Bargh, 1989). A common technique that meets this criterion is to measure interference of distracting stimuli as an indicator of automatic attention allocation (e.g., Eriksen & Eriksen, 1974; Shaffer & LaBerge, 1979; Theeuwes, 1996). In our experiments, positive and negative stimuli were presented as task-irrelevant distractor stimuli that participants should try to ignore in order to optimise their task performance. Attentional bias was measured via interference effects of these distractor stimuli. (2) We propose that certain types of goal or action contexts influence the operation of a *global* affective screening mechanism (i.e., automatic processing should be biased towards all kinds of information of a certain valence). This must not be equated with an increased accessibility of specific goal- or task-related information. Previous research has demonstrated an attentional bias towards stimuli that are directly relevant for goal pursuit or are related to the *specific* content of the goals and current concerns of a person (e.g., Newman et al., 1993; Riemann & McNally, 1995; for a review see Klinger, 1996). A large portion of this effect, however, is due to the fact that stimuli related to a current concern acquire subjective valence (Bock & Klinger, 1986; Klinger, 1996). It is thus important not to confound attentional biases in global affective parameters with goal- or task-specific effects mediated by valence. For that reason, attentional biases in global affective parameters must be determined by the help of stimuli that are in no way related to the goal or activity whose influence is to be analysed.

Overview of the experimental procedure and hypothesis

In the following experiment, a simple letter-naming task was used to analyse automatic attentional capture effects of chance and danger signals. In each trial, a target letter and a distractor letter were simultaneously presented on the screen. Following a technique developed by Derryberry (1993), rules for gaining and losing points were introduced. For each participant, one of the letters had a positive incentive value (*chance letter*) and one had a negative incentive value (*danger letter*). Whenever the chance letter was presented as the target stimulus, points could be gained by a fast naming of this letter but no points could be lost by a slow response. On the other hand, when the danger letter was presented as the target stimulus, points could be lost by a slow naming of this letter but no points could be gained by a fast response. The remaining letters were neutral (i.e., points could be neither gained nor lost). Attentional biases towards chance and danger signals were measured via the interference that the chance and danger letters produced when they were presented as distractors in the naming task. Interference effects can be attributed to automatic attentional processes. Throughout the experiment, the naming task was combined with a secondary visual detection task. The detection task served to induce a positive or negative action focus during the lottery announcement phases (see later).

Positive or negative goal orientations were induced repeatedly during the experiment by announcing lottery situations in which either money could be won immediately (*positive outcome focus*) or money could be lost immediately (*negative outcome focus*). After the announcement of a lottery, the combined naming and detection task had to be performed for some further time (*lottery announcement phase*). At the end of this time interval, the lottery game was carried out (see Figure 1 for an illustration of such a sequence). Moderating effects of positive and negative goal orientations on automatic affective attention were determined by analysing changes in the magnitude of the interference of chance and danger stimuli in the naming task during the announcement phases of the different lottery games. In order to keep the announced lottery game salient throughout these phases, the secondary detection task was now made relevant for the chances of the following lottery game. During the announcement phases, participants could influence their chances in the lotteries by fast or slow reactions in the detection task. In the *positive action focus* condition, participants could improve their chances in the lottery games by fast reactions in the detection task during the lottery announcement phases but chances could not deteriorate. In the *negative action focus* condition, slow

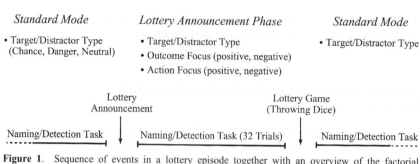

Figure 1. Sequence of events in a lottery episode together with an overview of the factorial manipulations in the standard task mode and during the lottery announcement phases.

reactions in the detection task during the lottery announcement phases led to a deterioration of chances in the lottery games but participants had no possibility to improve their chances. Goal and action focus manipulations do not relate in any way to the stimuli of the primary naming task that is used to measure automatic attentional biases. Moderating effects of these variables on attentional biases can thus be attributed to changes in global affective parameters.

With the present experiment, both of the major research questions that were sketched in the introduction can be addressed. A general asymmetry in attentional biases for positive and negative stimuli can be tested by comparing the interference for the chance and danger letters in the standard mode of the naming task. Additionally, the manipulation of goal and action focus during the lottery announcement phases allows a test whether these attentional biases are influenced by situational variables (i.e., current goal and action orientations).

METHOD

Participation

Forty-nine students (40 women, nine men; age mean was 21.5 years) from different faculties of the German Universities of Trier and Münster participated. The datasets of four persons were incomplete and had to be excluded because the experiment was terminated due to a winning or losing in the first lottery situation (see Procedure for further explanations). On average, participants received DM 10 (about US $6) for their participation (see later).

Materials

The upper-case letters K, P, T, and A were used as stimuli in the naming task. A letter was 5 mm high and 3 mm wide. The target letters were presented in light grey colour, whereas the distractor letters were presented in white colour. The background colour of the computer screen was black. For each participant, one of the letters signalled an opportunity to gain points (chance letter), another letter signalled the danger to lose points (danger letter), and the remaining two letters were neutral (i.e., no points could be gained or lost). Assignment of letters to the chance, danger, and neutral conditions was counterbalanced across participants.

Design

In the naming task, two variables were manipulated within subjects: *target type* and *distractor type*. All possible combinations of target letters (*target type*: chance, danger, neutral-1, and neutral-2) with distractor letters (*distractor type*: chance, danger, neutral-1, and neutral-2) were presented repeatedly during the experiment for each participant. Goal orientation was varied within subjects by announcing lottery games in which money could be either won or lost (*outcome focus*: positive vs. negative). For each participant, two positive and two negative lotteries were announced during the experiment. The order of the lottery games was counterbalanced across participants. Action focus during the lottery announcement phases was manipulated between subjects by the help of the secondary detection task (*action focus*: positive vs. negative). In the positive action focus condition, participants could increase their chances in the lottery games by fast detection reactions. In the negative action focus condition, chances in the lottery games could deteriorate by slow detection reactions.

Procedure

Participants had to appear at the laboratory twice. At the first arrival, each participant received DM 10, and an appointment was made for the experiment for the following week. Participants were informed that the experiment required them to participate in a game in which money could be either won or lost. We assumed that at the time of the experimental session participants had already spent the previously received money and thus should experience the experimental situation as a balanced one in which they could either win money or lose money of their own.[1] In the experimental session, participants were tested individually. Three practice blocks of increasing complexity were run to acquaint participants with the rules of the game. In a first block (1 minute), participants just had to practice the letter naming task without any reference to the rules of gaining or losing points. In the second practice block (5 minutes), the rules for winning and losing points in the naming task were introduced and the naming task was now combined with a secondary visual detection task (see later). At the end of the second practice block, participants had to reproduce the rules for winning and losing points in the naming task. If the rules were not reproduced correctly, the second practice block was repeated. In a third practice block (four minutes), the lotteries were explained and abbreviated versions of one positive and one negative lottery situation were simulated. After the third

---

[1] Apparently, this manipulation was quite successful. Some of the participants who lost the game even asked the experimenter what we would do with the money we got from them.

practice block the experiment was started. Participants had to work at the combined naming and detection task for 27 minutes. During the task, two positive (chance to win) and two negative (danger to lose) lottery games were conducted. The lotteries were announced after 4, 10, 16 and 22 minutes. Four participants won or lost in the first lottery game and thus had to be excluded from the data analyses because they did not provide data for the positive and negative *outcome focus* conditions. For 49 participants the dataset allowed a factorial analysis of the *outcome focus* factor. For four of these participants, the experiment was terminated after two lottery announcement phases, six participants won or lost in the third lottery, and for 39 participants, the experiment was terminated after all four lottery announcement phases had been carried out.

Rules for winning and losing money. Participants were told that if they ended the experimental task with a positive score (see later) they would win DM 10, otherwise they had to pay DM 10. Additionally, participants were informed that they could immediately win the DM 10 in each positive lottery game and that they could immediately lose the DM 10 in each negative lottery game irrespective of their actual score in the naming and detection task. In this case the experiment would be terminated immediately.

Lottery games. During the lottery games, a matrix of 6×6 squares was shown on the screen. In a positive lottery (positive *outcome focus*), some of the squares were green, in a negative lottery (negative *outcome focus*), some of the squares were red. The remaining squares were grey. Participants had to throw a die twice, the first number specified the row and the second number specified the column of the matrix. If the specified square was green or red the participants had won or lost, respectively. If the specified square was grey, the participant had neither won nor lost and the naming task went on as usual.

Lottery announcement phases. The lotteries were announced 32 trials before a lottery game was actually conducted. These 32 trials constitute the lottery announcement phase of a lottery. During the lottery announcement phases, all possible trials (4 targets $\times$ 4 distractors $\times$ 2 target positions) of the naming task were presented once in a randomised sequence. To avoid a confusion of the effects of *outcome focus* or *action focus* with attentional effects induced by feedback or a change in score, no points could be gained or lost in the letter-naming task during the lottery announcement phases. The word CHANCE (in green; announcement of a positive lottery) or the word DANGER (in red; announcement of a negative lottery) was shown in the top line of the screen, and the colour of the frame in which the stimuli of the naming task appeared was coloured green or red accordingly. Additionally, the matrix of 6×6 squares (see earlier) was presented at the beginning of each lottery announcement phase. As is evident from the logic of the game, the matrix indicates the actual chances for the upcoming lottery: The number of green squares signals the chance to win in a positive lottery. If all squares are green, the lottery will be won with certainty, if all squares are grey, there is no chance to win the lottery. The number of red squares signals the danger to lose in a negative lottery. If all squares are red, the lottery will be lost with certainty, if all squares are grey, there is no danger to lose the lottery. The chances in the lottery games could vary during the lottery announcement phases. The nature of these changes was determined by the factor *action focus*. For participants in the positive action focus condition, an additional green square was added or a red square was deleted whenever a *fast* reaction was given in the detection task during a lottery announcement phase. In this condition, the matrix initially contained no green square at the beginning of a positive lottery announcement phase, and six red squares at the beginning of a negative lottery announcement phase. During an announcement phase, six detection reactions were required. Because there was a 50% chance of a fast detection reaction (see later), participants ended up with approximately three green or red squares at the end of the lottery announcement phases. For participants in the negative action focus condition, an additional red square was added or a green square was deleted whenever they gave a *slow* detection reaction. In this condition, the matrix initially contained six green squares (positive lottery) or no red square (negative lottery). Again, because there was a 50% chance of a slow detection reaction (see later), participants also ended up with an average of three green or red squares. The number of coloured squares changed immediately after a fast (positive action focus) or slow (negative action focus) detection reaction had been registered. These changes were made salient to the participants by a short flicker of the coloured square that appeared or disappeared.

Rules of the naming task. Participants were informed that they could gain 10 points by a fast naming of a specific letter (the chance letter) whenever this letter appeared as the target letter but that no points could be lost by a slow response, and that they would lose 10 points by a slow naming of another letter (the danger letter) but no points could be gained by a fast response towards this letter. As a criterion to classify response latencies as fast or slow, the individual median of naming latencies of the previous 25 correct responses was used, that is, the criterion was constantly adjusted throughout the experiment. Response latencies below the median were classified as fast, response latencies above the median were classified as slow.[2] Some participants might have reached very high positive or negative scores during the experiment which might have

---

[2] Note that avoiding a slow response (which is the goal whenever a danger target appears) amounts to the same thing as producing a fast response (which is the goal whenever a chance target appears) because response latencies were classified as either fast or slow—there was nothing in between. Thus, differences in attentional effects for the chance and danger letters do not reflect a different amount of effort that is required to perform successfully in response to these stimuli rather than differences in the nature of the incentive value of these letters.

reduced suspense and dampened their motivation for an optimal performance. To prevent this, the time criterion was adjusted throughout the experiment in proportion to the current score. For each point above or below zero, 0.05 standard deviations of the latency distribution of the previous 25 trials of the naming task were subtracted or added to the median criterion. Maximal adjustment was ± 2 standard deviations. Above that, to ensure an overall reliable performance, 10 points could be lost by giving a wrong naming response or by giving an extremely slow response, regardless of the type of target letter. Naming latencies that were more than three interquartile ranges above the third quartile of the distribution of the previous 25 naming latencies (i.e., far out values; Tukey, 1977) were classified as extremely slow responses.

Rules of the secondary detection task.   Participants had to press a key as fast as possible when a small opening appeared in a frame in which the stimuli of the naming task were presented. In standard mode, two points could be gained by a fast detection reaction. A slow detection response or a false alarm (i.e., pressing the key when no opening appeared) led to a loss of two points. During the lottery announcement phases, fast and slow responses in the detection task determined the chances of winning and losing according to the *action focus* factor (see earlier). Fast and slow reactions in the detection task were determined by a simple time criterion (500 ms) that was continually adjusted 50 ms downwards or upwards after each fast or slow detection reaction, so the chances of a fast or slow detection reaction were kept at approximately 50% each throughout the experiment.

Procedural details of the combined naming and detection task.   All relevant stimuli and information concerning the combined naming and detection task were presented in a rectangular white frame that was visible throughout the experiment. The frame was 15 mm high and 30 mm wide and was posited in the upper half of the screen. The trials of the combined task consisted of the following sequence of events: Two white asterisks appeared side by side in the centre of the frame. After 750 ms, the asterisks were replaced by the target and distractor letters with a random determination of position. Then, participants had to name the target letter. Naming latencies were registered by a voicekey apparatus to the nearest millisecond realised by means of a microphone connected to a sound blaster audiocard. The letter stimuli remained on the screen until a response was registered by the voice key or five seconds had elapsed. In each trial, the target letter was presented to a second CRT screen allowing the experimenter to check the correctness of the response (i.e., incorrect naming or false triggering of the voicekey). Then the current score was shown in the middle of the frame. A plus or minus sign was shown in brackets behind the current score if points had been gained or lost in the last trial due to a fast or slow naming response. After 1750 ms, the score and the feedback sign were deleted from the screen and the next trial started without interruption. In some of the trials, a small opening (3 mm wide) appeared at a random position in the top or bottom line of the frame. The opening could appear during the presentation of the score or during the presentation of the asterisks but not during the presentation of the letter stimuli. After the maximum time to give a fast detection reaction, the opening was automatically filled again. As soon as participants detected an opening, they had to press a key on the computer keyboard. The sequence of events in a trial was the same for the standard mode and the announcement phases of the lotteries. In the standard mode of the task, all possible combinations of target and distractor letters were presented in a random order. The position of the target letter (left or right) was also randomised across trials. An opening appeared during a trial with a probability of 20%.

RESULTS

Mean reaction times for the naming task were derived only from those trials in which a correct response was given and no voicekey error occurred (98.1% of all trials). Trials in which a detection reaction was required were not included in the analyses. Reaction times below 200 ms (1.0%) or above 1000 ms (0.2% of all trials) were also discarded. Means were calculated for all combinations of target and distractor letters that comprised different letters. Latencies for neutral target letters with chance, danger, and neutral distractors were used to analyse interference effects. Note that even in the neutral baseline condition, target and distractor letter were not identical (i.e., the neutral condition already provides an estimate of response latencies in an incompatible condition). Interference due to chance (danger) distractors was calculated by subtracting the mean latencies of the neutral baseline condition from the mean of the combinations of a neutral target with the chance (danger) letter as a distractor. Facilitation due to the chance (danger) letter was computed similarly by subtracting the mean latencies of the neutral baseline condition (i.e., combination of a neutral target letter with the other neutral letter as distractor, see earlier) from the mean of the combinations of the chance (danger) letter as a target with a neutral distractor.[3] All variables were computed separately for the standard mode and for the four different types of announcement phases of the lottery (i.e., for the combinations of a positive/negative outcome focus with a positive/negative action focus). The data are summarised in Table 1.

---

[3] As already stated in the introduction, interference scores are the main dependent variable for the following analyses because they reflect an automatic (counterintentional) allocation of attention to the distracting stimuli. Facilitation scores for the valent target letters are reported as additional information. An interpretation of facilitation scores is ambiguous because they might reflect non-automatic processes (e.g., strategic response preparation).

TABLE 1

Mean naming latencies (in ms) for different combinations of target and distractor letters in different experimental conditions

	Distractor Neutral[a]		Target Neutral[a] / Distractor Neutral[a]	Target Neutral[a]		Interference scores[b]		Facilitation scores[c]	
	Chance	Danger	Neutral	Chance	Danger	Chance	Danger	Chance	Danger
Standard Mode (n = 49)	498	507	520	557	534	37 (5)	14 (3)	22 (6)	13 (7)
Positive outcome focus									
Positive action focus (n = 25)	528	538	540	562	562	23 (10)	23 (9)	12 (13)	2 (12)
Negative action focus (n = 24)	489	513	524	532	536	8 (9)	12 (11)	34 (9)	11 (10)
Negative outcome focus									
Positive action focus (n = 25)	517	540	542	586	547	45 (13)	5 (11)	25 (12)	2 (12)
Negative action focus (n = 24)	489	501	517	536	518	19 (8)	1 (10)	28 (10)	16 (11)

[a] Naming latencies for the neutral/neutral baseline condition were computed only for those trials in which two different neutral letters were presented.
[b] Interference score (SEs in parentheses) were calculated by subtracting the neutral baseline from the mean RTs for a neutral target with the valent distractors.
[c] Facilitation scores (SEs in parentheses) were calculated by subtracting the mean RTs for the valent targets with a neutral distractor from the neutral baseline.

Effects of chance and danger letters in standard mode.   Both the chance distractor, $t(48) = 7.28$, $p < .001$, and the danger distractor, $t(48) = 4.35$, $p < .001$, produced stronger interference than an incompatible neutral distractor letter in the standard mode of naming task. The interference was stronger for the chance distractors than for the danger distractors, $t(48) = 4.59$, $p < .001$. An analysis of facilitation scores revealed a similar (reversed) pattern of results. Naming latencies were shorter for the chance target, $t(48) = 3.95$, $p < .001$, and the danger target, $t(48) = 2.00$, $p = .05$, than for the neutral target letters. Again, the facilitation was slightly stronger for the chance letter targets, $t(48) = 1.70$, $p < .10$.

Moderating effects of outcome focus and action focus.   To estimate moderating effects of *outcome focus* and *action focus* on attentional biases, a 2 (Distractor Type) × 2 (Outcome Focus) × 2 (Action Focus) ANOVA was conducted for the interference scores that were measured during the lottery announcement phases. A main effect of *distractor type* was found, $F(1, 47) = 4.72$, $p < .05$. During the lottery announcement phases, interference for the chance distractor was generally stronger than for the danger distractor. This effect is further qualified by an interaction with *outcome focus*, $F(1, 47) = 4.70$, $p < .05$. Interference was stronger for combinations of *distractor type* and *outcome focus* that are of opposite valence (see Figure 2). Whereas interference of the chance distractor was stronger (though not significantly)

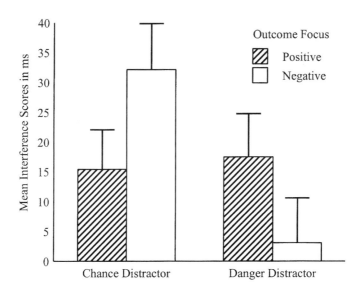

Figure 2.   Mean interference scores of chance and danger distractors as a function of a positive or negative *outcome focus*. Error bars reflect the standard error of the respective means.

when a negative lottery game was announced, $F(1, 47) = 2.88$, $p < .10$, the opposite numerical pattern emerged from the interference of the danger distractor, but $F(1, 47) = 1.79$, $p = .19$. All other effects were nonsignificant, in particular, a positive or negative action focus did not differentially influence the strength of the interference effects of the chance and danger distractors, $F < 1$.

In a corresponding 2 (Target Type) × 2 (Outcome Focus) × 2 (Action Focus) ANOVA for the facilitation scores a main effect of *target type* was found, $F(1, 47) = 8.13$, $p < .01$. Facilitation for the chance targets was generally stronger than for the danger targets. Above that, the three-way interaction just missed the conventional criterion of significance, $F(1, 47) = 2.84$, $p < .10$. When a positive lottery game was announced, facilitation for the chance target was slightly greater with a negative action focus than with a positive action focus, $F(1, 47) = 2.06$, $p = .15$, whereas in the other cases *action focus* did not influence the magnitude of the facilitation scores, all $Fs < 1$. All other effects in the analysis were nonsignificant.

DISCUSSION

Two results of the present experiment are especially important for the questions whether attention is allocated preferably to positive or to negative information and how stable such an asymmetry is. (1) Interference of the chance distractors was stronger than interference of the danger distractors although the naming task was completely balanced with regard to the probability and importance of winning and losing points: (a) the amount of points gained by a fast response to the chance target was equal to the amount of points lost by a slow response to the danger target, (b) chance and danger stimuli appeared equally often during the task, (c) winning and losing points was equally probable because the median of previous responses was used as a time criterion. This result is at variance with the assumption of a general attentional bias in favor of negative stimuli (e.g., Hansen & Hansen, 1988; Pratto & John, 1991). At least in some contexts automatic vigilance is biased towards stimuli signalling an opportunity to gain something. (2) Interference of chance and danger distractors was stronger after lottery games of the opposite valence had been announced. Attentional biases for stimuli with a positive or negative incentive value apparently depend on the actual goal orientation or outcome focus. In order to evaluate this finding, it is important to note that the manipulation of *outcome focus* was realised by announcement of either a positive or a negative lottery game which did not contain any reference to the stimuli or rules of the naming task. Any effects of this factor on attentional biases measured in the naming task must have been mediated by changes in *global* parameters of automatic affective processing. The finding thus supports the assumption that biases in the processing of valent information are not invariant but can be influenced by current goal and action orientations.

Although this finding is in line with the theoretical assumption that automatic attention allocation is of key importance to mediate between goals and information processing, the direction of the interaction effect in the present experiment was not expected. Somewhat surprisingly, announcement of positive and negative lottery games led to a relative strengthening of automatic vigilance towards stimuli of the opposite valence. At least two different interpretations of this incongruence effect can be advanced. The most straightforward interpretation is to take the direction of the interaction effect at face value and to postulate a genuine affective incongruence effect. Incongruence effects of mood on automatic affective processing were already reported by Derryberry (1993). Allocating attentional resources to mood-incongruent information might be functional for the regulation of emotion and action. At least for negative mood states, this is a highly plausible assumption. Allocating attentional resources to positive information in a negative mood might be important for mood repair (Isen, 1984; Taylor, 1991; Taylor & Brown, 1988). Affective incongruence effects might also support processes of a reorientation towards new goals and incentives after failure (Brandtstädter & Rothermund, in press; Rothermund, 1998). An affective incongruence mechanism might thus be necessary for a flexible switching of attention between opportunities and dangers.

On the other hand, the incongruence effect of the present experiment might also have occurred as a result of an inverse internal coding of the lottery games. Because the probabilities of winning and losing in the lottery games were rather small (on average, the chances were 1/12), participants might have coded the positive lottery as a low chance (i.e., as a chance that will probably be missed), and the negative lottery as a harmless danger (i.e., as a danger that will easily be warded off). Alternatively, participants might have experienced the announcement of the negative lottery as a signal to fight against this danger and increase their vigilance towards opportunities to avoid the potential loss. Similarly, announcing a lottery in which participants could win the game might have alerted participants not to miss this opportunity, which increased their vigilance for potential danger signals. In these cases, the observed interaction of outcome focus and distractor valence is interpreted as an affective congruence effect because interference was strongest for the distractors that would correspond in valence to the internal coding of the lottery games.

The data of the present experiment do not allow a definite decision between these conflicting interpretations, that is, further research will have to address the question of whether the affective attention system functions according to a congruence logic, an incongruence logic, or both. Whatever the correct interpretation of the incongruence effect of this experiment will turn out to be, the present result provides unambiguous support for our central hypothesis, that is, for the assumption that the automatic affective attention system is open to the regulating influence of the current goals and actions of a person. In addition, the paradigm that is introduced in this article will prove to be a flexible tool to answer some of the questions relating to the interplay of attention, motivation, and cognition.

Manuscript received 7 May 1999
Revised manuscript received 28 September 1999

REFERENCES

Bargh, J.A. (1989). Conditional automaticity: Varieties of automatic influence in social perception and cognition. In J.S. Uleman & J.A. Bargh (Eds.), *Unintended thought* (pp. 3–51). New York: Guilford Press.

Bargh, J.A. (1997). The automaticity of everyday life. In R.S. Wyer (Ed.), *Advances in social cognition* (Vol. 10, pp. 1–61). Mahwah, NJ: Erlbaum.

Bock, M., & Klinger, E. (1986). Interaction of emotion and cognition in word recall. *Psychological Research, 48,* 99–106.

Brandtstädter, J., & Rothermund, K. (in press). Intentional self-development: Exploring the interfaces between development, intentionality, and the self. In L.J. Crockett (Ed.), *Nebraska symposium on motivation: Current theory and research in motivation* (Vol. 47). Lincoln, NE: University of Nebraska Press.

Brandtstädter, J., Wentura, D., & Rothermund, K. (1999). Intentional self-development through adulthood and later life: Tenacious pursuit and flexible adjustments of goals. In J. Brandtstädter & R.M. Lerner (Eds.), *Action and self-development: Theory and research through the life-span* (pp. 373–400). Thousand Oaks, CA: Sage.

Brendl, C.M. (1997). *Annäherungs-Vermeidungsmotivation und Einstellungen implizit messen? Geschwindigkeit von Armstreckung versus Armbeugung* [Speed of arm extension versus arm flexion: Implicitly assessing approach/avoidance motivation and attitudes?]. Paper presented at the 6th Social Psychology Meeting, Konstanz, Germany.

Brendl, C.M., Higgins, E.T., & Lemm, K.M. (1995). Sensitivity to varying gains and losses: The role of self-discrepancies and event framing. *Journal of Personality and Social Psychology, 69,* 1028–1051.

Cacioppo, J.T., Priester, J.R., & Berntson, G.G. (1993). Rudimentary determinants of attitudes: II. Arm flexion and extension have differential effects on attitudes. *Journal of Personality and Social Psychology, 65,* 5–17.

Chen, M., & Bargh, J.A. (1999). Consequences of automatic evaluation: Immediate behavioral predispositions to approach or avoid the stimulus. *Personality and Social Psychology Bulletin, 25,* 215–224.

Derryberry, D. (1988). Emotional influences on evaluative judgments: Roles of arousal, attention, and spreading activation. *Motivation and Emotion, 12,* 23–55.

Derryberry, D. (1989). Effects of goal-related motivational states on the orienting of spatial attention. *Acta Psychologica, 72,* 199–220.

Derryberry, D. (1993). Attentional consequences of outcome-related motivational states: Congruent, incongruent, and focusing effects. *Motivation and Emotion, 17,* 65–89.

Derryberry, D., & Tucker, D.M. (1994). Motivating the focus of attention. In P.M. Niedenthal & S. Kitayama (Eds.), *The heart's eye* (pp. 167–196). San Diego, CA: Academic Press.

Draine, S.C., & Greenwald, A.G. (1998). Replicable unconscious semantic priming. *Journal of Experimental Psychology: General, 127,* 286–303.

Eriksen, B.A., & Eriksen, C.W. (1974). Effects of noise letters upon the identification of a target letter in a nonsearch task. *Perception and Psychophysics, 16*, 143–149.

Gollwitzer, P.M., & Moskowitz, G.B. (1996). Goal effects on action and cognition. In E.T. Higgins & A.W. Kruglanski (Eds.), *Social psychology: Handbook of basic principles* (pp. 361–399). New York: Guilford Press.

Greenwald, A.G., Draine, S.C., & Abrams, R.H. (1996). Three cognitive markers of unconscious semantic activation. *Science, 273*, 1699–1702.

Hansen, C.H., & Hansen, R.D. (1988). Finding the face in the crowd: An anger superiority effect. *Journal of Personality and Social Psychology, 54*, 917–924.

Hansen, C.H., & Hansen, R.D. (1994). Automatic emotion: Attention and facial efference. In P.M. Niedenthal & S. Kitayama (Eds.), *The heart's eye* (pp. 217–243). San Diego, CA: Academic Press.

Higgins, E.T. (1996). Ideals, oughts, and regulatory focus: Affect and motivation from distinct pains and pleasures. In P.M. Gollwitzer & J.A. Bargh (Eds.), *The psychology of action: Linking cognition and motivation to behavior* (pp. 91–114). New York: Guilford Press.

Isen, A.M. (1984). Toward understanding the role of affect in cognition. In R. Wyer & T. Srull (Eds.), *Handbook of social cognition* (Vol. 3, pp. 179–236). Hillsdale, NJ: Erlbaum.

Kahneman, D., & Tversky, A. (1984). Choices, values, and frames. *American Psychologist, 39*, 341–350.

Klinger, E. (1996). Emotional influences on cognitive processing, with implications for theories of both. In P.M. Gollwitzer & J.A. Bargh (Eds.), *The psychology of action: Linking cognition and motivation to behavior* (pp. 168–189). New York: Guilford Press.

Markus, H., & Nurius, P. (1986). Possible selves. *American Psychologist, 41*, 954–969.

Markus, H., & Ruvolo, A. (1989). Possible selves: Personalized representations of goals. In L.A. Pervin (Ed.), *Goal concepts in personality and social psychology* (pp. 211–241). Hillsdale, NJ: Erlbaum.

Murphy, S.T., & Zajonc, R.B. (1993). Affect, cognition, and awareness: Affective priming with optimal and suboptimal stimulus exposures. *Journal of Personality and Social Psychology, 64*, 723–739.

Newman, J.P., Wallace, J.F., Strauman, T.J., Skolaski, R.L., Oreland, K.M., Mattek, P. W., Elder, K.A., & McNeely, J. (1993). Effects of motivationally significant stimuli on the regulation of dominant responses. *Journal of Personality and Social Psychology, 65*, 165–175.

Peeters, G., & Czapinski, J. (1990). Positive-negative asymmetry in evaluations: The distinction between affective and informational negativity effects. In W. Stroebe & M. Hewstone (Eds.), *European review of social psychology* (Vol. 1, pp. 33–60). Chichester, UK: Wiley.

Pratto, F. (1994). Consciousness and automatic evaluation. In P.M. Niedenthal & S. Kitayama (Eds.), *The heart's eye* (pp. 115–143). San Diego, CA: Academic Press.

Pratto, F., & John, O.P. (1991). Automatic vigilance: The attention-grabbing power of negative social information. *Journal of Personality and Social Psychology, 61*, 380–391.

Riemann, B.C., & McNally, R.J. (1995). Cognitive processing of personally relevant information. *Cognition and Emotion, 9*, 325–340.

Rothermund, K. (1998). *Persistenz und Neuorientierung: Mechanismen der Aufrechterhaltung und Auflösung zielbezogener kognitiver Einstellungen* [Persistence and reorientation: Maintaining and dissolving goal-related cognitive sets]. Unpublished doctoral dissertation, University of Trier, Trier, Germany.

Rothermund, K., Wentura, D., & Bak, P. (1995). *Verschiebung valenzbezogener Aufmerksamkeits-asymmetrien in Abhängigkeit vom Handlungskontext: Bericht über ein Experiment.* [Shifting of attentional biases to valent stimuli in different action contexts: Report of an experiment]. *Trierer Psychologische Berichte, 22 (4)*.

Rothermund, K., Wentura, D., & Bak, P. (1996). *Automatische Vigilanz: Aufmerksamkeitsbindung durch verhaltensrelevante soziale Informationen* [Automatic vigilance: Attention allocation to behaviour-relevant social information]. *Trierer Psychologische Berichte, 23 (1)*.

Shaffer, W.O., & LaBerge, D. (1979). Automatic semantic processing of unattended words. *Journal of Verbal Learning and Verbal Behavior, 18,* 413–426.

Solarz, A.K. (1960). Latency of instrumental responses as a function of compatibility with the meaning of eliciting verbal signs. *Journal of Experimental Psychology, 59,* 239–245.

Taylor, S.E. (1991). Asymmetrical effects of positive and negative events: The mobilization-minimization hypothesis. *Psychological Bulletin, 110,* 67–85.

Taylor, S.E., & Brown, J.D. (1988). Illusion and well-being: A social psychological perspective on mental health. *Psychological Bulletin, 103,* 193–210.

Taylor, S.E., & Gollwitzer, P.M. (1995). Effects of mindset of positive illusions. *Journal of Personality and Social Psychology, 69,* 213–226.

Theeuwes, J. (1996). Perceptual selectivity for color and form: On the nature of the interference effect. In A.F. Kramer, M.G.H. Coles, & G.D. Logan (Eds.), *Converging operations in the study of visual selective attention* (pp. 297–314). Washington, DC: American Psychological Association.

Tukey, J.W. (1977). *Exploratory data analysis.* Reading, MA: Addison-Wesley.

Wentura, D., Rothermund, K., & Bak, P. (2000). Automatic vigilance: The attention-grabbing power of approach- and avoidance-related social information. *Journal of Personality and Social Psychology, 78,* 1024–1037.

Williams, J.M.G., Watts, F.N., MacLeod, C., & Mathews, A. (1997). *Cognitive psychology and emotional disorders* (2nd ed.). Chichester, UK: Wiley.

Zajonc, R.B. (1980). Feeling and thinking: Preferences need no inferences. *American Psychologist, 35,* 151–175.